This Stops With Me

Recovering From the Abuse of a Narcissistic Mother and Making Sure You Don't Become One

Louise Grayhurst

All effort has been executed to present accurate, up to date, reliable, complete information. No warranties of any kind are declared or implied. Readers acknowledge that the author is not engaged in the rendering of legal, financial, medical or professional advice. The content within this book has been derived from various sources. Please consult a licensed professional before attempting any techniques outlined in this book.

By reading this document, the reader agrees that under no circumstances is the author responsible for any losses, direct or indirect, that are incurred as a result of the use of the information contained within this document, including, but not limited to, errors, omissions, or inaccuracies.

Table of Contents

To my magnificent tribe: my husband, dad and beloved children.
I hit the love jackpot having you in my life!
Thank you for your love.

Acknowledgments

To my darling husband: You have been a constant in my life, even when I pushed you away in my tumultuous years when I was trying to figure this heady stuff out. You stayed and loved me unconditionally, even from the time-out sidelines. You were there, unwavering in your love. From our start, you always recognized and knew my worth, even when I dismissed it. You are my all.

To my dad: Thank you for never turning your back on me, even when I was under my mother's control. You took each hit and criticism silently, internalizing it and thinking it was you, but it wasn't. It was her. I have relished our years together and the way you are so involved and included in my family's life. I love the way you and hubby get on so well and that you are, in fact, the only guest who can stay in my home indefinitely. Thank you for being my dad in this life. You were just what I needed so that I could be me.

To my readers: I wish you well on your beautiful journey. I would love to hear your stories of newly found freedom and self-love. You can reach me at:

- Email: louisegrayhurst@gmail.com
- Instagram: louisegrayhurst

I would also like to thank Carol McGregor, my trauma-informed practitioner, whose expertise has been instrumental in my healing journey. Carol specializes in anxiety, depression, and lingering emotional effects from illness. With her guidance, I have been able to reframe the story of my life and embrace a future filled with ease and grace.

Carol McGregor's Healing Approach

Carol McGregor resides in Sydney and works internationally online with clients. She uses a structured and compassionate approach to help clients address unresolved and distressing events from their past. This process involves a series of steps tailored to meet individual needs, employing deep imagination and body-centered techniques to facilitate healing and transformation. You can find out more about Carol McGregor as follows:

- Website: https://www.carolmcgregorintegrativetherapy.com

- Email: carolmcgregor@iprimus.com.au

- Facebook:
  https://www.facebook.com/CarolMcGregorIntegrativetherapy.com

- Instagram: https://www.instagram.com/carolmcgregorinsta

Disclaimer: The healing journey described in this book is based on the personal experience of Louise Grayhurst and may not represent typical outcomes. This therapeutic process should be conducted by a qualified practitioner.

Introduction

I remember standing in my mother's shower some years back when I was around 30 years old, visiting her home in the UK. My son was about three years old and my daughter was a baby. My mother's bathroom door didn't lock, and I stood there naked, with my recovering postpartum body, enjoying an afternoon shower in peace.

Sylvia, my mother, never knocked. She came in, and instantly I felt more than naked; I felt stripped. I jokingly asked her to leave, saying I'd be out in a minute, but my mother always believed that her children were her possessions and that she had the right to access us whenever, wherever.

She told me that she was "my mother" and didn't need to leave the bathroom. She proceeded to look at me while making idle conversation. I was not respected as a 30-year-old woman trying to have a private shower while my young children napped. My mother clearly viewed my body as an extension of hers, and my feelings and embarrassment did not matter to her.

I stood there feeling like an ashamed four-year-old: naked, disrespected, and overruled. If this were a courtroom, there stood the meanest judge who abused her power and thrived on it. That was my life back then.

Thinking back to the woman I was, standing in that shower—a new mom, a budding lawyer, a new wife, a scared and deflated daughter—I don't recognize that "old me." Some years back, after going through a journey probably similar to what you, the reader, may be going through now, I decided that I deserved better. That I *was* better and that I needed to leave my mother and start a new life—and be happy.

When my trauma therapist told me about her program, she said that if I "did the work" I would experience a sense of happiness like never before. I thought that sounded so pie-in-the-sky. I didn't know happiness. I didn't know mental and emotional clarity. Instead, I knew self-doubt, anger, searing hurt entwined with rage; I knew I didn't know who I was or why I felt so awful.

Before I went on my healing journey, I tried many different antidepressants and sleeping tablets, had therapists, visited psychics. I sobbed, silently screamed, scribbled in my journals, slammed the evening dishes into the sink, and even cried to an unsuspecting church minister. My friends knew about my mother; my husband couldn't understand the depth of my pain, and my children sensed I was "emotionally somewhere else."

My body experienced it, and I gained weight through tucking into cheesecakes and pies. I couldn't work out why I felt so grim, so mentally split, so fractured.

My mom even appeared in my dreams. I would grind my teeth at night and often had dreams where I was screaming at her, my chest burning with rage. In the morning, my husband would ask me what I had been dreaming about because I'd been kicking him in my sleep.

Because of the way my mother raised me—with caution, disapproval, and, sometimes, vengeance—I must have unnerved something in her when I came into her life as her daughter. I must have reminded her of something or someone deep in her psyche. Or she may have been threatened by my confidence, my feisty spirit.

Thankfully, that is in the past. I moved on.

I have two teenagers, a son and a daughter, and I always teach my kids that knowledge is power. So, about six years ago, after I'd read a few articles about narcissism and toxic moms that seemingly matched up to my mother's behavior, I then read some more. I recognized the traits and realized that trauma can be many things. It can stem from a single stressful event or an extended period of stress caused by an oppressor, leading to patterns of abuse.

Once I had recognized these traits in my mother and understood how they were impacting my life on every level, I made a concerted effort to find a way out of my pain and suffering. This journey eventually led me to investigate therapy and various other modalities that could help me uncover and release the emotional baggage, leading to freedom.

This book is not a self-pity fest where we, as daughters, lick our wounds from these insufficient mothers. It's a book about being real about what we go through and having the bravery to stop the beliefs and change our behavior going forward.

Reading a book like this means you want to change and find peace and freedom from negative patterns in your life. Rediscovering yourself and changing old beliefs isn't easy, but it's worth it. You may scream your lungs out along the way, feel sick to your stomach, or even decide to get off. You may think you'll always feel this way. But remember, all roller coasters end. At some point.

I have been "sober" from my mother for six years now. I do not drink her poison or crave her contact. I am indifferent to her being. Before that, I "broke up" with her a few times. Really, it is like an intimate, abusive relationship. I specialize in domestic violence law, and going through a family divorce is tough.

I do not think of her on Mother's Day. In fact, when asked about my mother, I feel a sense of peace and calm in my head and politely say, "I don't have a mom." Because I don't. My mother "died emotionally" a long time ago. Now, on Mother's Day, I celebrate myself and how proud I am that my son, daughter, and step-kids love me in a pure, uncomplicated way.

It stopped with me. And it can stop with you.

As a survivor of a narcissistic mother, I understand the profound impact this type of emotional abuse can have. The journey to healing and self-discovery is challenging but worthwhile. In this book, I share my personal experiences and research-based insights into narcissistic personality disorder (NPD) and its effects on children.

NPD is characterized by an inflated sense of self-importance, a need for excessive attention, and a lack of empathy. Are you nodding your head in recognition? Then I don't need to tell you that when a parent has NPD, it can devastate their children. A study in the *Journal of Child and Family Studies* found that children of narcissistic parents are more likely to experience depression, anxiety, and low self-esteem (Dentale et al., 2015). These children often feel inadequate, unworthy, and emotionally neglected and struggle with boundaries, relationships, and asserting their needs.

Growing up with a narcissistic mother involves manipulation, gaslighting, and emotional blackmail, leading to deep emotional wounds. As adult daughters, breaking free from this toxic dynamic requires courage, self-awareness, and the willingness to confront painful truths. However, with the right tools and support, healing and building a life of authenticity and self-love is possible.

This book explores the characteristics of narcissistic mothers, their impact on us, their children, and strategies for healing. We will delve into the latest research on NPD, share personal stories, and provide guidance and hope for those on this journey. By understanding NPD, we can break the cycle of abuse and create a brighter future.

Together, we will explore self-discovery, boundary setting, and emotional resilience. We will learn to trust our instincts, cultivate healthy relationships, and build fulfilling lives. Most importantly, we will understand that we are not alone, and that healing is possible.

I know you. I've been you. You're a woman who doesn't give herself enough credit. You're smart, caring, and naturally beautiful, but you often feel misunderstood and carry wounds from a broken heart. You likely bought this book to understand why you feel the way you do. You know something is off in your life. Maybe you feel fractured or carry a sadness that makes you cry at random times and in random places. You want to learn why your mother is so hurtful and how to change your life.

I see you reading this book in the bath, on your commute, or in bed with tea. You could be anywhere in the world; what matters is that you're an emotionally intelligent woman seeking answers. If I were near you, I'd give you a gentle squeeze and whisper, "Well done; you're being brave."

This is hard stuff. I've been there too, desperate to understand my mother's awfulness and dysfunction. I, too, wanted to recognize her traits, learn about her issues, and start believing new things about myself.

Chapter 1:

I Am Your Mother

One must be a sea, to receive a polluted stream without becoming impure. –
Frederich Nietzsche

Narcissism exists on a complex spectrum, touching relationships and lives in varying degrees of intensity. At its core, it's more than just self-love or vanity—it's a pattern of behaviors and traits that can manifest in subtle to severe ways. While some individuals may display occasional narcissistic tendencies in specific situations, others embody these traits so deeply that they shape every relationship they form.

The hallmark traits of narcissism—grandiosity, a need for admiration, and a lack of empathy—ripple through all relationships, whether parental, romantic, professional, or platonic. At work, a narcissistic boss might take credit for their team's successes while blaming others for their own failures. In friendships, they might dominate conversations and react with hostility when they don't receive constant attention. In romantic partnerships, they often cycle between idealization and devaluation of their partner.

But perhaps nowhere are these traits more damaging than in the parent-child relationship, where the impact shapes a child's entire developmental journey. In this dynamic, the parent views their child not as an individual with their own needs and desires, but as an extension of themselves - a mirror to reflect their own perceived greatness or a vessel to fulfill their unmet dreams.

In fifth grade, there was a girl at school, Bianca, who had the shiniest, silkiest blonde hair. Her legs were smooth, her clothes smelled of the loveliest detergent, and her mom doted on her. She just smelt like love. She glowed. I felt like a small dragon next to her, longing for the same kind of love and attention from my own mother. But my mother was different; she was a narcissistic parent, displaying traits of NPD, a mental health condition characterized by an inflated sense of self-importance, a deep need for admiration, and a lack of empathy for others. I now know that NPD affects an estimated 1% of the general population, with rates slightly higher in men than in women (Stinson et al., 2008). But at the time she was just my mom, the human being assigned to be my parenting mentor for this earthly life. Next to Bianca's mom, my mom was emotionally glitched. Loving her was like trying to hug cut glass. Sometimes, I would get an injury, and sometimes, I would avoid a stab wound.

I would watch Bianca's mom pick her up from school and casually chat with the other mothers. If Bianca wanted to do guitar lessons or sports, her mom would tenderly and actively take an interest. I wished I was Bianca, getting picked up from school every day by an uncomplicated, doting, and loving mother, whisked away back home to a place where I could be a child. I felt like I got a dud. My mother lacked empathy, one of the hallmarks of narcissistic parenting. She was unable to tune into my emotions and needs, instead focusing on her own wants and expectations, leaving me feeling unheard, unseen, and invalidated. Children of narcissistic parents often experience this kind of emotional neglect, as their parents prioritize their own needs over those of their children (Weir, 2014).

I observed a lot of my friends' mothers over the years. They seemed normal—so loving, and genuinely interested in their daughters. My mother didn't interact with me like that; it was different. It was a functional relationship. Duty over care. My mom told me she loved me, and was even encouraging in some ways, but her actions spoke louder than her words. As an attorney specializing in domestic and family violence, I know about abusive relationships. My relationship with my mother was like being pushed down the stairs, then getting blamed for tripping, before being handed an ice pack for my broken ribs! She was highly controlling, using manipulation and guilt to keep me in line, setting unrealistic standards and expectations, and becoming angry or dismissive when I failed to meet them. I lived in constant anxiety and fear, and learned to walk on eggshells around her to avoid triggering her wrath. These behaviors are consistent with the patterns of emotional abuse often observed in narcissistic parenting.

Outsiders looking in will view these mothers as devoted and self-sacrificing. In my family, I even believed my mother loved me for a while. I perpetuated the "perfect mother" propaganda and fiercely defended her to anyone who questioned her. I wrote her love notes and thanked her for being the best mom, telling her how lucky I was to have her. I was brainwashed, and so were my siblings. My mother needed admiration and validation and viewed me as an extension of herself, taking credit for my accomplishments and basking in the reflected glory. But she was quick to criticize or belittle me when I fell short, reinforcing the message that my worth was contingent upon my ability to make her look good. This pattern of idealization and devaluation is a common dynamic in narcissistic families, as the narcissistic parent seeks to maintain control and bolster their own fragile sense of self.

I couldn't love her the right way, though, like so many other daughters in relationships like this. I was known as the needy child, the draining child, or the spirited one. I loved her too much or not enough. It was always something. It didn't matter how well I did at school, how educated I was, or what qualifications I had; my mere existence seemed to irk her. Growing up in this environment had far-reaching consequences. I struggled with trust issues, having learned that love is conditional and can be withdrawn at any moment. I had difficulty setting boundaries and asserting my own needs, having been taught that my feelings and desires were secondary to those of my mother. Adult children of narcissistic parents are more likely to experience depression, anxiety, and low self-esteem, as well as difficulties in forming healthy relationships—all things I recognize in myself.

I didn't need a wicked stepmother to poison me. If I were Snow White, my own mother would have been baking cupcakes with the juice of the poisoned apple, and once I had passed out, she would have been doing the Heimlich on me! It was a yo-yo relationship that shaped my attachment style and led to difficulties in forming healthy, secure relationships in adulthood. And I'm not alone in experiencing this: Children raised by narcissistic parents often develop insecure attachment styles, such as anxious or avoidant attachment, which can impact their ability to form stable, trusting relationships later in life.

To complicate matters in my case, my mother was also a high-functioning alcoholic. A counselor by day at a private hospital, she was well-respected among the doctors and nurses. But at home, she was an unhinged dog always ready to snap at her puppy, who seemed to be a little too challenging. Healing from the wounds of her narcissistic parenting has been a complex and ongoing process, involving learning to recognize and challenge the distorted beliefs and patterns of behavior that were instilled in me during childhood. From my research, I know that a combination of individual therapy, support groups, and self-help strategies can often be effective in helping adult children of narcissistic parents heal from their experiences and develop healthier coping mechanisms. And I certainly needed support from a range of sources as I walked my own healing path.

It was hard to comprehend how a person who was supposed to love and adore me was actually the person causing me to feel so fractured on the inside. One of the most important steps in my healing journey has been learning to cultivate self-love and self-acceptance. As the child of a narcissistic mother, this has been a challenging task, as I had internalized the message that I was fundamentally flawed or unworthy. And again, I know that my experience is not unique: Developing self-compassion and learning to recognize and challenge negative self-talk are crucial components of healing for adult children of narcissistic parents.

In our family, there were four of us as siblings. I was the youngest. And each of us got a different version of my mother growing up. It has been crucial for me to surround myself with supportive, nurturing relationships, setting boundaries with toxic family members, seeking out therapy or support groups, and building a chosen family of friends and loved ones who offer unconditional love and acceptance. The experts back me up here: Having a strong support network and engaging in healthy relationships can help mitigate the long-term effects of narcissistic parenting.

My eldest brother and sister got phase one Sylvia. The canteen-serving, mothers' committee volunteer, family Christmas hostess type of mom.

My younger brother and I missed that one; we got phase two "revolution" Sylvia, when she was going through her reimaging, crusade phase. She went back to university and studied psychology, drank red wine excessively, divorced my dad, and became a single mom who had more boyfriends than I had teenage pimples.

She achieved wonderfully in her career; she was even on a radio talk show as the resident agony aunt. I would sit next to her while troubled callers phoned in asking to speak to this "wonderful woman." I would go with her every Monday night as her companion and support. The radio DJ commented to me after one show that he loved to watch me watch my mother because I had so much admiration for her.

I did. I loved her with all my beating heart.

But she was the type of mother who would tell you how useless you were, but that she was sure you had the skills to improve.

My mother's narcissism, like that of many others, wasn't confined to her role as a parent. It colored every relationship she formed—with her colleagues, her friends, her romantic partners, and even herself. The same patterns of control, manipulation, and emotional unavailability that defined her parenting also manifested in her professional relationships and personal friendships. This consistency across different spheres of life is typical of narcissistic personalities—the core traits remain constant, though the individual might wear different masks depending on the audience and context.

My mom. It was an exhausting, clusterfuck of a semi-conditional relationship that started at birth and ended when I broke up with her at 35 years of age. Welcome to Narcissism 101.

Chapter 2:

What's Her Style?

One of the subjects I'm involved with in the Criminology school at my university is "Understanding Domestic and Family Violence." This course doesn't touch on the legal aspects but rather focuses on the psychology behind the abuser and how there are many different typologies that make up these fractured people. In one of our prescribed textbooks, *Why Does He Do That?: Inside the Minds of Angry and Controlling Men* by Lundy Bancroft (2003), the author sets out the various male abuser profiles and mythologies. The book explores how an abuser might blame his toxic childhood, how he may have been scarred by his mother, how his previous partner hurt him, or that he abuses those he loves the most. Excuses. Excuses. Abuse is abuse.

The Victim Card

The book also mentions that an abuser can have different typologies and mythologies in how he manipulates and abuses his partner. It's a brilliant read, and I recommend it for anyone wanting to learn more about that topic. But it also reminds me that toxic parents can imbue different styles or methods of achieving control.

I have seen through cases in family court how some parents play the victim card to their children to garner their support during a child custody conflict. Similarly, some parents, particularly mothers, use this method in other areas of life too. For example, my mother used the victim card to make us feel so guilty and sorry about her own suffering as a child. She told us about her childhood abuse from a very young age, and we felt dreadful. She made her past our future by dumping her trauma on us. We felt vengeful for her and so fiercely protective over her past suffering—especially when she introduced us to these family members in our childhood.

She portrayed herself as a "survivor" of childhood trauma and, because of her terrible experience, we were her "gifts." We would somehow free her by being her children. So, we were always held by her guilt around her early childhood trauma. And although she didn't mention it to us often, it was well-known and hung thick in the air. She used this "rite of passage" as a hold over us in a number of different ways.

The Dictator's Guise

Her style was dictatorship, absolute control, under the guise of being a Mary Poppins mother who only had our best interests at heart. Actually, she only had her own best interests at heart. Her style was to control, not to allow free spirits or anything that she felt was out of her comfort zone. So, little girls like me, who could assert themselves from a young age, or who loved to be boisterous like her brothers, or who loved her father, were something to be reined in. My mother said I was too spirited and that she would do her best "to love it out of me." What a sin that was; in essence, I was just being my beautiful, authentic young self.

Guilt, Manipulation, and Gaslighting

My mother also used guilt and manipulation to gaslight anyone who resisted her. She would plant seeds of doubt that took such a deep root that our minds became poisoned soil. False beliefs that benefited her and crushed us were seeded all the way through our lives, even into adulthood. She was a wicked farmer of our minds, using comments like:

- "Is that how you want to treat your mommy? After all I do for you?"

- "Don't disappoint me; it's the worst thing you can do." Followed by, after the incident, "You disappointed me terribly. Why do you act like this?"

And after she'd emotionally abused us or manipulated the hell out of us and placed the heavy weight of guilt on us (I'm surprised we could walk), she would say something like, "It's all over now; come give me a love," or "Mommy forgives you."

The Art of Breaking a Child's Spirit

Narcissistic mothers are master architects of their children's self-doubt, systematically grooming them from an early age to become compliant vessels for their own needs and desires. This grooming process is calculated and insidious—they plant seeds of inadequacy so early that these beliefs become foundational to the child's sense of self.

By the time the child is old enough to start forming their own identity, these toxic messages are already deeply embedded in their unconscious mind. "You're too sensitive," "You're not as smart as your sister," "Why can't you be more like the other kids?"—these aren't just casual criticisms, they're carefully crafted tools of control. The mother knows that a child who believes they are fundamentally flawed is easier to manipulate and control.

This grooming serves a specific purpose: creating a child who is "broken in," much like how one might break the spirit of a wild horse. A child who doubts their own worth, capabilities, and perceptions is more likely to seek their mother's approval, comply with her demands, and accept her distorted version of reality. They become perfect extensions of their mother's ego, unable to distinguish their own desires from what their mother has programmed them to want.

In my case, my mother groomed me to believe I was "too spirited"—a label often given to creative, energetic children who think and behave outside conventional norms. These children tend to be naturally enthusiastic, independent thinkers who don't easily conform to mainstream expectations. But rather than celebrating these qualities, my narcissistic mother saw them as character flaws that needed correction, simply because she couldn't comprehend or relate to a child who didn't fit neatly into her narrow worldview. She labeled me as different, odd, and problematic—even suggesting I had learning difficulties—rather than acknowledging that my "out-of-the-box" nature simply didn't align with her rigid expectations. While any genuine concerns about learning or behavioral challenges should be properly assessed, in this case, she wasn't seeking to understand or support me; she wanted to reshape my very essence into something more manageable for her. By making me question my natural temperament, she created a deep-seated insecurity that made me more susceptible to her manipulation.

These early seeds of self-doubt become the foundation upon which narcissistic mothers build their control. What makes this form of emotional grooming particularly devastating is how it hijacks the child's natural developmental process. Instead of building healthy self-esteem and autonomy, the child develops a distorted self-image that serves the mother's needs. They learn to see themselves through their mother's warped lens, internalizing her criticisms as fundamental truths about their identity.

The Narcissist's Lack of Accountability

One of the most striking characteristics of a narcissistic mother is her inability to admit fault or apologize. The word "sorry" was rarely, if ever, part of my mother's vocabulary. I now know that this lack of accountability stems from a deep-seated lack of empathy and an unwillingness to acknowledge the feelings and experiences of others, especially her children. A narcissistic mother may justify her hurtful actions by claiming that she was only trying to help or that her child is too sensitive. She may even go so far as to blame her child for her own emotional outbursts or manipulative behavior, further compounding the emotional damage inflicted upon the child.

Gaslighting, which I mentioned above, is another common tactic employed by narcissistic mothers. When confronted with their hurtful or manipulative behavior, they will often deny, minimize, or reframe the situation in a way that makes the child question their own perceptions and feelings. This can lead to a deep sense of self-doubt and confusion. Just like my siblings and I did, the child begins to wonder if they are the problem, rather than the mother's toxic behavior.

If we ever confronted our mother about a hurtful comment or action, she would respond by saying something like, "You're too sensitive,"

"That never happened," or "You're remembering it wrong." Over time, this constant invalidation of our experiences, a phenomenon known as "gaslighting," meant we began to doubt our own reality and even started to believe that we were the ones with the problem.

Gaslighting isn't just a problem in the moment; it can have severe long-term effects on a child's mental health and sense of self. It can lead to chronic self-doubt, anxiety, and depression, as well as difficulty trusting your own perceptions and intuition. In extreme cases, gaslighting can even lead to a complete breakdown of the child's sense of reality, leaving them vulnerable to further manipulation and abuse.

At the core of a narcissistic mother's behavior is a fragile and inflated ego that requires constant feeding. My mother would overinflate her own importance, portraying herself as a long-suffering, selfless martyr who had sacrificed everything for her children. This narrative served to guilt us, her children, into compliance and admiration, while also shielding her from any criticism or accountability.

However, as an adult I can see that beneath this grandiose facade lay a deep sense of insecurity and emptiness. A narcissistic mother's sense of self-worth is often dependent on external validation, whether that comes from her children's compliance, her social status, or her professional achievements. This need for constant validation creates a bottomless pit of emotional hunger that can never be truly satisfied, leading to a constant cycle of manipulation and emotional abuse. Her children may feel like they are walking on eggshells, never quite sure what will trigger her wrath or disapproval. I remember as a young teenager feeding our dogs; I dropped the dogs' bowls, and the food spilled onto the floor. Unknowingly, I glanced at my mom, who was cooking in the kitchen. I didn't think I was upset or frightened, but my mother remarked that I looked scared of her and asked me, so lovingly, "Why would you be scared of me?" On a conscious level, I didn't think I was. I was programmed to believe she was a lovely mother.

Chronic emotional stress like this can have long-lasting effects on a child's mental health and self-esteem, making it difficult for them to form healthy relationships and set boundaries later in life. Children of narcissistic mothers often struggle with a range of emotional and psychological challenges, including low self-esteem, chronic guilt and shame, difficulty trusting others, and a tendency to gravitate toward unhealthy or abusive relationships. They may also struggle with codependency, as they have learned to prioritize the needs and emotions of others over their own.

As I reflect on the behavior of these mothers and their patterns, I find myself observing from a place of compassion, rather than disbelief, my mother's struggle to express love unconditionally. The simplicity of love, devoid of any conditions or manipulations, is something I've come to appreciate deeply, especially as I witness the pure love I have for my own children.

My ability to love freely stems from my journey of learning to love myself. While moments of disbelief may still arise, I refuse to let them overshadow the lessons I've learned. Instead, I hold onto the wisdom gained from recognizing my mother's insecurities and imperfect love. I'm grateful for the clarity it has brought me, guiding me in how I choose to nurture and cherish my own family.

Turning that experience into a source of empowerment, I now stand as a guardian, shielding my children from any negative influences. Just as I witnessed abused women seeking refuge from toxic relationships, I recognize echoes of my mother's traits in those who perpetuate such cycles.

In considering my siblings' experiences, I see the impact of our upbringing manifesting in various ways. While each of us had the same mother and we all now have children of our own, only one of us has embarked on a journey of healing and liberation. The scars borne by my siblings are evident in their parenting styles and personal struggles. Yet, I see them as individuals navigating their own paths, still finding their way to emotional growth and fulfillment.

Though they tolerate our mother's criticisms and maintain a strained relationship with her, I understand their reluctance to confront her. It's a reflection of the deep-seated fear instilled in them since childhood, a fear of asserting themselves and setting boundaries. Despite the challenges they face, I hold onto hope for their continued growth and healing. Each step they take toward self-awareness and empowerment is a testament to their strength and resilience.

Chapter 3:

The Good Mother Disguise

Childhood trauma, such as sexual abuse, can have long-lasting effects on an individual's mental health and well-being. We know that childhood sexual abuse is associated with increased rates of depression, anxiety, and substance abuse in adulthood, and that childhood sexual abuse is a significant risk factor for the development of psychopathology in adulthood, including personality disorders (Fergusson et al., 2013).

This was certainly the case for my mother. She had a dark past and a rotten childhood. She was abused in the worst way, abandoned, and placed in care; her brothers were equally abused. None of those three siblings ever broke the generational curse, and they either died from alcoholism or carry a heart filled with darkness and an inability to love.

Despite this trauma, my mother declared to anyone who would listen that by having her four children, she was miraculously healed from the hurt of her childhood. She believed that being a mother "saved her." But, in reality, it triggered her. And as we all got older, we became the bullets in her gun—especially me.

She did not give us many details of the abuse. We know it was sexual, and that she witnessed her mother and brothers being physically abused. To cope, my mother developed what I call the "Mary Poppins mother-in-disguise" persona. Her tactic to survive was to block out her pain through alcohol and never admit the truth about how her childhood was too painful for her to even think about. Mom then grew this super strong ego, where she was this brilliant, self-sacrificing woman and a loving and unaffected mother, and you couldn't criticize her because she couldn't handle it.

These "Mary Poppins mothers-in-disguise" love to present a picket-fence life, but actually, they build barbed wire fences where their children cannot play. They often use guilt as a manipulation tactic, especially if they are unwell or a single mother. They will remind you how hard they work for you or how sick they feel, making it difficult for you to express your own needs or feelings without feeling guilty (Efthim et al., 2001).

Children who grow up with this type of inner guilt and who focus on their mother's struggles are not celebrated as individuals. Nor are their personal struggles recognized. Eating disorders, problems with friends and fitting in, or academic worries are glossed over. Moms like mine don't allocate time and energy to their children's worries, and they are not tender with their children's feelings and individual needs. In our family, growing up under Sylvia's control, we were not four individuals, growing up and finding our place in the world. Rather, we were just some sheep in her herd. We were "her offspring," humans who were birthed by her and who would owe her an allegiance for all our days.

Manipulation is another common trait of narcissistic mothers, who may use emotional blackmail, guilt-tripping, or gaslighting to control their children and maintain their idealized image (Dentale et al., 2015). By playing the victim, these mothers can elicit sympathy and support from others, further reinforcing their narrative of being the sacrificial, devoted parent. If you're the daughter of one of these mothers, you will know all about this trait. They wear their troubles and struggles on their sleeves for all to see. It is part of their identity, being this wholesome, sacrificing mother for the benefit of their "beloved" children.

This was certainly true of my mother. She decided late in life to study psychology. I admired her for that; in fact, I thank her for always pushing us to study further after school and go to university. But my mother never went to a counselor or psychologist for help with her past trauma. She said that through studying psychology, she was fine. No, she wasn't.

She had significant trauma, and she needed to deal with it. I wish she had done so, because she might have cleared some of her emotional blockages and false beliefs, and she could have gone on to be a more grounded and kinder person. Her refusal to seek professional help despite her painful past points to narcissistic traits of denial and an inflated ego. My mother didn't want to do the hard work of facing her trauma. That emotional work, that hard slog, is tough stuff, and that's why most people don't do it. We end up with "repeat offenders" in this life, who think that just by growing older, things will get better or they will miraculously wake up and find "peace." No, babe. Peace comes after a hard-fought war, usually within ourselves.

Narcissistic mothers often emphasize the importance of family, which is ironic. They tell everyone that "family" is everything to them and how family must stick together. However, this proclamation is usually a means to maintain control and ensure that their children remain loyal and compliant. In reality, just as I described earlier, a narcissistic mother's idea of family is one that revolves around her own needs and desires, with little regard for the emotional well-being of her children (Day et al., 2019). Her need to have a "close" family is to build a strong defense unit with unfailing and unquestioning supporters.

This is the most confusing belief to disprove. You may find that your siblings and extended family struggle to believe you when you explain that this false identity of your mother's is a twisted lie based on control, not unconditional love. It may have also taken you many years to work out that family, friends, and lovers can proclaim that they love you and you are their world; however, in reality, the proof of this proclamation is all in their actions, not their words.

A mother who has perpetuated this front has a lot to hide. My husband knew me from a young age and knew of our family. He often remarked that he thought our family was "so close" and our mother was "so devoted." He grew up in awe of our well-put-together family. Throughout our marriage, he tried hard but couldn't quite grasp the depth of my mother's destruction and the extent of the lie that she presented to the world. She was always so complimentary to him and said I was important in her life.

Over the years, my husband was in disbelief at how my siblings treated me and ganged up in support of my mother when I resisted her control. It was brutal. These were brilliant disguises that had been cemented and played out for years. My siblings still battle with this idea that our mom was not a good and loving mother who had our best interests at heart. They would probably say that "she didn't know any better" or "her childhood tainted her focus" or that "she was doing her best as a single mom, working so hard." Those are nothing but excuses for abuse.

I don't dispute her hardworking nature; in fact, I admired that about her. I dispute that her abuse was covered up and that her work, childhood experiences, and whatever else was an excuse for poor behavior and emotionally damaging parenting. However, my siblings still remember "the sacrifices," the tears of my mother, and her long soliloquies about how hard her life had been and how she was the savior of our family against my father. As the late Queen Elizabeth II said, "Recollections may vary."

The "good mother disguise" is a complex and insidious facade that narcissistic mothers often employ to maintain their idealized image and their control over their children. To the outside world, these mothers may appear loving, devoted, and self-sacrificing—just like my husband believed my mother to be—but behind closed doors, they engage in a pattern of emotional abuse and manipulation that can have devastating effects on their children's mental health and well-being.

One of the hallmarks of the good mother disguise is the ability to present a flawless public image. A narcissistic mother may be heavily involved in her children's school activities, volunteer for community events, or cultivate a wide social circle, all while presenting herself as the epitome of maternal devotion. However, this public persona is often a carefully crafted mask designed to hide the dysfunction and abuse occurring within the family (Kacel et al., 2017).

Behind this mask, a narcissistic mother engages in a variety of manipulative and abusive behaviors designed to maintain her power and control over her children. One common tactic, which you may well recognize from your own experience, is the use of guilt and shame to manipulate children into compliance. Your mother may remind you of her sacrifices, her hardships, or her physical and emotional pain, making you feel responsible for her well-being and happiness. This emotional blackmail can be particularly effective on children, who are naturally inclined to seek their mother's approval and love (Efthim et al., 2001).

As we touched on in the previous chapter, another tactic employed by narcissistic mothers that you might be familiar with is the use of gaslighting. This is a form of psychological manipulation in which the abuser attempts to sow seeds of doubt in the victim's mind, making them question their own memory, perception, and sanity. A narcissistic mother may deny or minimize abusive events, twist the truth, or rewrite history to suit her narrative. Over time, this constant invalidation of the child's experiences can lead to a deep sense of confusion, self-doubt, and emotional instability (Gunderson & Lyons-Ruth, 2008). As the children of these mothers, we grow up doubting ourselves and unable to make sense of our own judgment.

I can particularly relate to this from my final year of studying law at university, when I was experiencing extreme anxiety. On one occasion before a big exam, although I didn't know at the time, I was having a panic attack. My mother (despite her background in psychology) said I was suicidal and, of course, spread the word along the family grapevine, with no support coming forth from my Sylvia-trained siblings. I wasn't living with Sylvia then, but all I needed was a loving mom to come over, have a cup of tea with me, and encourage me to talk about my fears with her on an evening walk around the block. I needed love. Not condemnation and shame.

After I had finished my exam, I distinctly remember walking through the university gardens in the late afternoon sunshine. I phoned my mother straightaway, elated as I felt it had gone well, and physically relieved after I had vomited from anxiety. Sylvia, being herself, sliced through my joy and relief and said, "All that fuss and drama for nothing. You put me through hell yesterday." My anxiety was her inconvenience.

The way a narcissistic mother uses manipulation and abuse is often rooted in her own unresolved childhood trauma and emotional wounds. Just like my mother, many narcissistic individuals experienced abuse, neglect, or emotional deprivation in their early years, leading to the development of maladaptive coping strategies and a fragile sense of self. In the case of a narcissistic mother, she may project her own pain and trauma onto her children, who become targets for her unresolved anger, fear, and insecurity.

The impact of growing up with a narcissistic mother can be profound and far-reaching. As children of narcissistic parents, we are at increased risk for a range of mental health issues, including depression, anxiety, post-traumatic stress disorder (PTSD), and personality disorders (Dentale et al., 2015). We may struggle with low self-esteem, chronic feelings of guilt and shame, and difficulty trusting others, all of which can impair our ability to form healthy, intimate relationships in adulthood (Day et al., 2019).

One of the most insidious effects of narcissistic parenting is the way in which it can distort a child's sense of reality and self. Growing up in an environment where our feelings and experiences are consistently invalidated, as children of narcissistic mothers we may learn to doubt our own perceptions and intuition, leading to a phenomenon known as "narcissistic fog" (Yip et al., 2018). This fog can make it difficult for us as adults to recognize and break free from the patterns of abuse and manipulation we experienced in childhood, perpetuating the cycle of dysfunction and suffering.

The narcissistic fog acts as a veil, obscuring our ability even as adults to clearly see the harmful dynamics that shaped our upbringing. This lack of clarity can lead to a continued acceptance of toxic behaviors and relationships, as we may struggle to distinguish between healthy and unhealthy patterns of interaction. The fog may also contribute to feelings of self-doubt, causing us to question the validity of our own emotions and experiences, further reinforcing our narcissistic mother's control over our lives.

Moreover, the narcissistic fog can make it challenging for us to establish and maintain healthy boundaries with our narcissistic mother and other family members once we reach adulthood. The fear of confrontation, coupled with the ingrained belief that we are responsible for our mother's happiness, can keep us trapped in a cycle of trying to please and appease our narcissistic parent, even at the cost of our own well-being. This perpetuates the dysfunction and suffering throughout our lives, as even as grown-ups we continue to prioritize our mother's needs over our own, sacrificing our happiness and self-worth in the process.

It's normal to feel that learning about these traits is a complex and emotional process. Some of you may have prior knowledge of these traits and behaviors, while for others, reading about them may cement your suspicions and provide the missing puzzle piece. However, it can still be unnerving and may stir up emotions, making you feel quite wired. It's important to remember that confirmation of your mother's inappropriate behavior is not a reflection of you as a person.

Don't be afraid of learning. Gaining knowledge about emotions and how to change old self-beliefs is like acquiring a new skill for work. Many people study further at a university or enroll in an accredited course to learn a new skill or take on a new profession, with the goal of bettering themselves. This active pursuit of new understanding may not always be easy, and the subject matter may be challenging, but investing time in yourself is essential for personal growth.

Similarly, view this phase of your life as an opportunity to learn a new skill about yourself. Focus on understanding your past so that it doesn't dictate your future. Ask yourself: What do you want the outcome to be for your life?

It is never too late to understand something, even if it is unpleasant, and to reshape your experience by directing what you have learned into something positive.

It's likely that your mother was a control freak, and that you have become accustomed to conditioning your responses and lifestyle choices to keep her satisfied. The empowering aspect of this journey is that you are taking the lead in your life and re-establishing the power dynamics. This topic will be further discussed later in the book.

Only for your eyes
Your journals sit comfy on your shelf
the morning light shining its warmth on them.
All your laughter, tears, fears and love crushes sit neatly on the pages.
They sit so tight in a bundle, thick and bulging with your life stories.
The pages are like spells ready to come alive.
I love the way you trust me not to read them.
I love the way I don't want to.
I clear away your empty teacup left on your desk.
Your privacy is sacred to me.
It heals the pieces in me that were spied on growing up.
Your journals sit comfy on your shelf
the morning light shining its warmth on them.
All your laughter, tears, fears and love crushes are left only for your eyes, safely on the pages
-Louise Grayhurst

Chapter 4:

Mommy Knows Best

Parental alienation is a poisonous tactic that some parents use, often in the midst of a divorce or separation, to turn their children against the other parent. This can involve badmouthing the other parent, limiting contact, or even convincing the child that the other parent is dangerous or doesn't love them. The effects on children can be devastating, leading to confusion, guilt, and damage to the parent–child relationship that can persist into adulthood.

In family law practice, it's not uncommon to witness seemingly loving parents inadvertently causing harm to their children by projecting their unresolved issues with their former spouse onto their kids, instead of treating that relationship as a separate entity. During my family dispute mediation training, a retired family court judge emphasized to us, as mediators, that "Divorce won't kill your kids, but conflict will." This statement highlights the detrimental impact of ongoing parental conflict on children's well-being.

One of the most toxic manifestations of this conflict is parental alienation, which can be likened to a slow-acting poison that erodes the child's relationship with one of their parents. Parental alienation occurs when one parent actively undermines the child's relationship with the other parent, often through manipulation, false accusations, or portraying the targeted parent in a negative light. This behavior not only damages the child's bond with the alienated parent but also has far-reaching consequences for their emotional and psychological development.

The Manipulative Mother in Disguise

Some years back, I took my daughter to see the Disney movie *Tangled*, which puts a new spin on the classic fairy tale *Rapunzel*. In the movie, a wicked woman kidnaps Rapunzel as a baby and raises her in a tower, pretending to be her loving mother. However, the real reason is that Rapunzel has magical hair that keeps the woman young and beautiful. There's a haunting scene where the woman sings a manipulative song called "Mother Knows Best," guilting Rapunzel into believing that, no matter what, everything she does is out of love—even imprisoning and isolating her from the world. It was a sickening display of gaslighting, but I saw it for what it was: abuse. And it reminded me so much of my own mother, Sylvia.

As I sat in the darkness of the movie theater, I realized that there were two stark realities. I recognized the character on the big screen all too well. The experience I'd had with her in the past came back as a strong reminder of how I'd had the courage, just like the little girl in the movie, to break free and leave the tower. I sat there as a mother but also as the wise and brave girl who had grown up and moved on.

Meanwhile, my little girl beside me, munching on her popcorn, was happily watching a fun movie with her mommy, completely unaware of the deeper meaning behind the story. Thankfully, she does not recognize that crooked woman on the screen and does not have her as a mother in her own life, and never will. She's got me.

A Father's Unconditional Love

My father was the parent I was closest to growing up. He supported my interests, like when he bought me my first bird feeder after seeing how much I loved nature. Even though he couldn't tell a pigeon from a duck, he took me on bird-watching trips and guided walks through the mountains near our home. He did things like that throughout my life, and still does them to this day.

But my parents' 23-year marriage was awful. Sylvia used me and my siblings, especially the older ones, as de facto marriage counselors. She constantly complained to us about how unhappy she was and how our dad was the source of all of our family's problems. In her distorted view, he was uneducated, simple, a useless father and husband, bad with money, and someone she needed to divorce. She reminded us of the list of my father's faults so often that she might as well have written it as a grocery list and stuck it on our fridge.

The reality was that my dad is a kind man who always wants to help others. He is, however, emotionally vulnerable and too trusting, and he never should have married my mother. Rather than standing up for himself, he would bottle up his feelings until they erupted in bouts of temper. He never hurt us, but Sylvia turned us kids against him nonetheless.

For me to love my father and have a special bond with him was something my mother couldn't tolerate. For years leading up to their divorce, she told everyone that she was just waiting until I started high school to leave my dad, because she knew how close he and I were and that I "wouldn't handle the divorce well" as such a "daddy's girl." The implication was that she was suffering and delaying the inevitable split just for my sake, and it made my siblings resent me for prolonging the tension in our household. Everyone thought Sylvia was being such a doting, self-sacrificing mother, but I knew better.

Growing up, I witnessed firsthand the devastating impact of parental alienation. My narcissistic mother, consumed by her need for control and validation, systematically eroded my relationship with my father. Through a campaign of manipulation, false accusations, and emotional blackmail, she effectively turned me against him, leaving me confused, guilt-ridden, and torn between two worlds. The psychological damage inflicted by her selfish actions would reverberate throughout my life, manifesting in struggles with trust, self-worth, and interpersonal relationships.

And it's not just me. Research has confirmed the severe and long-lasting consequences of parental alienation, with children caught in the cross fire of their parents' conflicts at a higher risk for depression, anxiety, and substance abuse issues that can persist into adulthood. As I navigated the turbulent waters of my own experience, I came to understand the insidious nature of narcissistic mothers and their propensity for engaging in this emotionally destructive behavior. Their intense need for loyal children and their desire to be seen as the superior parent drives them to manipulate and undermine, leaving lasting scars on the very souls they should be nurturing (Bernet et al., 2020).

It is crucial for family law professionals, mental health practitioners, and parents to recognize the signs of parental alienation and take steps to intervene and protect the well-being of the children involved. This may include therapy, co-parenting education, and legal measures to ensure that children have the opportunity to maintain healthy relationships with both parents, free from manipulation and psychological harm.

The healthiest situation for children is to have the love and involvement of both parents, as long as the relationships are not abusive. Daughters especially need that bond with their fathers. I've seen the damage firsthand in my work as a family law attorney. Clients going through a divorce sometimes brought their children to consultations, which I felt was inappropriate, even though I understood when a mother in crisis had no other childcare options for a baby or toddler. But school-aged kids should never be exposed to these adult conversations and emotions. They pick up on everything and will internalize it if they hear one parent badmouth the other.

My mother once brought me to a meeting with her divorce lawyer when I was 13. It was embarrassing and the male attorney seemed uncomfortable, but he trusted that she knew what she was doing by involving me. Unfortunately, that trust was misplaced.

The Narcissistic Mother's Divide and Conquer Strategy

In addition to turning children against the other parent, narcissistic mothers often engage in another destructive tactic: sibling alienation.

Narcissistic mothers need allies in the family to feed their egos and maintain control. With her bottle of red wine in one hand and a loudspeaker in the other, my mother was like an army commander employing guerrilla warfare tactics. A key strategy was assigning labels to each of us four kids: the black sheep, the underachiever, the messiah who could do no wrong, and Peter Pan, the lost boy.

Narcissistic mothers love to assign roles to their kids. It's like they're the director of their own twisted family drama and we're all just playing the parts they've given us. These roles have nothing to do with our individual strengths or personalities. No, it's all about what serves mom's needs and keeps her in control.

Let's break down these roles. First, we have the "golden child." This is the kid who can do no wrong in mom's eyes. They're the shining example, always meeting her expectations and basking in her praise. But trust me, it's not all it's cracked up to be. The golden child is expected to be an extension of mom, sharing her every belief and attitude. Step out of line? Prepare for a major guilt trip. It's a heavy burden, especially if you're the eldest. You're suddenly mom's second-in-command, the sibling leader.

In my family, my eldest brother was the alpha male, the golden child. My younger brother? He was constantly overshadowed, despite having this amazing talent for mediating conflicts. But those skills were never recognized or celebrated—it was all about my older brother. My second brother was a diamond lying in the rough. Undiscovered.

Then there's the "scapegoat." If the golden child is mom's little angel, the scapegoat is the family punching bag. This poor kid can never seem to catch a break and takes the blame for everything that goes wrong. They face constant criticism, belittling, and sometimes even physical abuse. It's no wonder they often rebel against mom's authority.

And let's not forget the "invisible child." This kid copes by fading into the background, becoming the family peacemaker. They avoid conflict at all costs, but while this might help them survive in the short term, it can lead to some serious self-esteem and relationship issues down the line.

But why does mom bother with all these labels? It's simple—it allows her to create her own little support system within the family. By turning some siblings against others, she always has someone to take her side, no matter how hurtful her actions might be to the others. In my family, my mother loved to play the victim, the struggling single parent. My dad? He was painted as the villain. And when I dared to feel empathy for him, I was kicked out of mom's loyal sibling club.

At the end of the day, all this role-assigning stems from the mom's desperate need for control and validation. By dividing us and keeping us at odds with each other, she maintains her power and ensures we're too busy navigating the family drama to question her authority. It's a classic narcissistic parent move: divide and conquer. And it's scary how well it works at keeping all of us under her emotional control.

I was the black sheep, the scapegoat, the "difficult," "attention-seeking" child whose strong spirit needed to be broken. As I got older, the narrative shifted to calling me "odd" and questioning my mental health. I have seen in legal practice in domestic violence cases how the abuser often spins a mental health narrative on the abused victim when he feels that she may be "winning" in a family law dispute. Sylvia divided us, gossiping and complaining behind our backs about our life choices and any relationships she disapproved of. For someone who preached about the importance of family, she certainly didn't hesitate to pit us against each other.

She also needed at least one of my siblings, or my dad, on her "team," loyal soldiers who saw her as the righteous one and me as the problem. It gave her power and weakened my ability to resist her control. This is a hallmark of narcissistic parenting: systematically isolating and scapegoating the child who challenges the parent's authority.

The Psychology of Family Brainwashing

The psychological impact of parental and sibling alienation runs deeper than most people realize. It's akin to being raised in a fundamentalist religious household, where every aspect of your reality is filtered through a specific belief system. Research shows that children of narcissistic parents internalize their parents' distorted worldview as reality, similar to how children in highly controlling religious environments internalize religious beliefs as absolute truths (Shaw, 2014).

Think about what it means to question your religious upbringing when it's been the foundation of your entire existence—your family relationships, your moral compass, your understanding of the world. Now imagine the psychological upheaval required to challenge a narcissistic parent's carefully constructed reality. The stakes are equally high, the emotional toll just as devastating.

The brainwashing becomes deeply embedded in the child's psyche because it starts so early and is reinforced by the entire family system. Studies indicate that even as adults, many siblings remain trapped in their assigned roles, their inner child still desperately seeking the narcissistic parent's approval (Verrocchio & Baker, 2015). Breaking free requires more than just recognizing the dysfunction—it means dismantling your entire understanding of family, love, and self-worth.

This is why many adult children of narcissists, even when they recognize the toxicity, choose to maintain the status quo. Baker and Ben-Ami (2011) found that the emotional energy required to challenge the narcissistic parent's reality is enormous, and the backlash can be severe. The narcissistic parent views any challenge to their authority as a direct threat, responding with rage, manipulation, or complete rejection. Meanwhile, siblings who remain under the parent's influence often join in the attack, desperately trying to maintain the family system they've known their entire lives.

Research shows that this dynamic creates a form of trauma bonding within the family unit. According to Waikamp et al., (2021), the siblings who remain aligned with the narcissistic parent often exhibit symptoms similar to those seen in cult members: an inability to question authority, black-and-white thinking, and an intense fear of rejection by the group. They've learned that survival depends on maintaining their position within the narcissistic parent's hierarchy.

The Damaging Impact of Sibling Alienation

The impact of sibling alienation can be just as damaging as that of parental alienation. Siblings who have been manipulated to gang up on another sibling end up with higher rates of depression, anxiety, and paranoia, in addition to difficulty trusting others and forming healthy relationships. Meanwhile, being ostracized and belittled by your siblings, with a parent's encouragement, can lead to long-term self-esteem issues and resentment that sabotages sibling relationships well into adulthood (Dantchev et al., 2019).

I would say that the bullies I faced in my childhood and into early adulthood, other than my mother, were my siblings. Like in my relationship with Sylvia, there were warm moments, but the default always prevailed and the warm seasons of love usually stopped whenever I asserted myself against Sylvia or voiced criticism of her. My siblings and I lost out on so many years of love and being carefree together because of Sylvia's doing.

Some narcissistic mothers will even extend their campaign outside the immediate family, turning grandparents, aunts and uncles, or family friends against the child they're targeting. The more people they can convince that the child is "difficult" or "troubled," the more validated they feel in their distorted worldview. This can leave the alienated child feeling completely alone and questioning their own reality.

As the family scapegoat, I've had to work hard to break free from my mother's toxic influence and the negative labels that were put on me. It's an ongoing journey, but I've learned that I deserve so much better—we all do. No child should have to fight so hard for a parent's love or be made to feel responsible for the dysfunction in their family. The blame lies squarely with the parent who manipulated and harmed them, not with the child they so wrongly alienated.

Growing up, my siblings and I were all brilliant little kids with our own strengths and vulnerabilities. Unfortunately, I do not look back fondly on my memories of growing up with them. I don't like having photos of that time in my home as I remember how difficult it felt.

My siblings were unawakened and emotionally shut down, living in survival mode, not recognizing the division our mom was creating among us. They did not want to rock the boat. As my defiance grew over the years, my siblings became a solidified hunting pack that included my mom. I felt bullied and judged in my own home, especially because I loved my dad so much. I simply did not fit in.

My liberal views were squashed and discussed behind my back as problematic and rebellious. I acted out in chaos and sought validation in the wrong places. My decisions were bold and fearless. I understand my behavior now and the reasons behind it. It would have been a comfort if any of my older siblings had taken me aside and asked, "What's really going on? Are you okay?"

After many years of snide remarks and half-baked efforts at love from them, I decided this family was not for me—not just my mom, but my siblings too. I was used to being on my own, both emotionally and physically, so breaking up with them was unfortunate but necessary.

They took a strong line against me when I silenced my mother and removed her from my life. None of them approached me to ask my side of the story. They could criticize dad, and I respected their views, but I wasn't allowed to ask probing questions or draw attention to mom's behavior.

After many years of living my life without siblings, and hearing of my nieces and nephews being born but not knowing them, I was contacted and told that my sister needed serious help. No one, not even my psychologically learned mother, had fully realized the extent of my sister's misery and the danger she was in living with her husband. The signs were there, but no one had asked my sister what was really going on.

It took me one phone call with my estranged sister, my former bully, to realize she was in an abusive, coercive, controlling marriage and battling severe depression. As we chatted on the video call, I could see she was constantly snacking on food, and I recognized her anxiety screaming out for help. The gaslighting was extreme; she had married a male version of our mother. History was repeating itself.

Suddenly, I went from not having these three people in my life to welcoming them back on my terms. It turns out the black sheep, a domestic violence and family law attorney with an eye for picking out perpetrators, wasn't so useless after all.

Having them back in my life had to be carefully negotiated. I worked with my trauma counselor to address how and why I would do this. It was bumpy, but I wanted to learn and progress. Thankfully, everyone seemed to have matured and was open to learning why I had walked away.

My sister, the biggest bully and mom's right-hand daughter, cried in a heartfelt apology as we sat on a beach in New Zealand talking about our childhood. She apologized for not protecting me as the older sister and for believing everything our mom said. A week later, I helped her pack up and move out of her marital home, leaving behind a dreary past.

Nowadays, I embrace my nieces, babysit them, and attend their school concerts, happily sitting next to their parents. I get "best aunty" drawings and clay-modeled hearts. It grounds me, knowing I did the work to heal the hurt and manage the future on my terms. Being an aunt to all my siblings' children gives me such warmth in my heart.

Some of my siblings may still not have healed within themselves, but that's their journey, not mine. For me, the most important thing is having a new relationship with them based on mutual respect. I forgave them for my sake, but I won't forget how far I had to come and why.

Chapter 5:

Green-Eyed Monster

My mother was my first jealous lover. –Barbara Grizzuti Harrison

As the mother of two teenage children, an 18-year-old son and a 15-year-old daughter, I have experienced the joys and challenges of raising both genders. When my son, my firstborn, came into the world, I didn't know what to expect as a boy mom. However, being a mother to a son was an absolute delight. He is now a gorgeous, intuitive, and emotionally sharp young man, and I love watching him grow up.

Narcissistic mothers, however, often struggle with their children growing up. They thrive on being needed by their children for everything, so as their kids develop their own opinions, tastes, and beliefs, these mothers feel threatened. The healthy detachment that well-adjusted parents encourage terrifies narcissistic parents, as they fear losing their identity and control over their children's lives.

Raising a son is often described as the slowest breakup a mother will ever experience. As they grow, they naturally need their mothers less, which can be a grieving process for any parent. I've experienced this myself, watching my son develop his own political and religious views as well as a clear idea of what he wants to do after school. While I may see potential shortfalls, I trust that he has what it takes to succeed on his own terms. Gone are the days when he would sit under my desk as I studied for my law exams. Now, I jump at the opportunity to spend any time with him, even if it's a late-night drive to McDonald's in my pajamas and slippers, where our conversations reach from friends and politics to mental health. As we drive back home, he says, "Take the long way home, Mom." And my heart melts. I cherish whatever time I have with him and let him venture into the world at his own pace.

Narcissistic mothers often view their daughters as direct competition and potential rivals in beauty, popularity, career success, marriage, wealth, and parenting. Sons, on the other hand, may not trigger the same level of threat due to their biological differences. In some cases, sons may even become protective of their mothers, depending on the family dynamic. The concept of the Oedipus complex suggests that mothers may seek their sons' attention, especially when they feel replaced by girlfriends or wives. Controlling mothers may attempt to cut off their sons' close friendships or romantic relationships out of fear of abandonment and jealousy of being upstaged.

Daughters born to narcissistic mothers face a particularly challenging road. Their mere existence as women can either unnerve their mothers or cause them to be overlooked entirely. If a daughter's natural qualities, such as her hair, body shape, or popularity, outshine her mother's, the mother may feel threatened and attempt to knock her daughter down to a more manageable level.

I experienced this firsthand during my teen years. At a random BBQ for family and friends one evening, my mother brought up my virginity and how I was such a good girl, questioning whether I would need to go on the contraceptive pill. I was sitting right there at the table, humiliated. I was 16 or 17 years old. The other mothers, just as pathetic as my own was, all chimed in about whether they could trust me or not to maintain my virginity. My mother had no respect for me as a young woman. My body and my sexual learning experiences were fodder for conversation at a BBQ. It was her way of getting me into line—and sending me a warning shot not to disappoint her by sleeping with my long-term boyfriend of three years. My mother put such guilt and shame around sex on me.

The impact of these kinds of experience at the hands of a narcissistic mother can be devastating and far-reaching. As daughters of narcissistic mothers, we may struggle with a distorted view of our own sexuality, feeling ashamed of our desires or believing that sex is dirty or wrong. This can lead to difficulties in forming healthy romantic relationships and expressing our sexual needs.

My mother's key tools as a parent were control, guilt, and shame—again, traits I am sure many of you will recognize. The burden of guilt and shame that daughters of narcissistic mothers carry can be immense, affecting our beliefs about sex, our body image, our relationships with food, and our ability to succeed in life. These deeply ingrained beliefs can remain in the subconscious mind until a conscious effort is made to change them.

As a parent, it is crucial to foster a healthy relationship between our children and their bodies, encouraging open communication and empowering them to make their own choices. I teach my children now that it is their body, their choice. I have guided them as much as I can, telling them about safety and the need to protect their bodies and their feelings, but I would rather they had a healthy relationship with sex and their bodies than associate such a pleasurable thing as sex with shame. By breaking the cycle of control, guilt, and shame, we can help our children develop a strong sense of self and the ability to form healthy, fulfilling relationships.

The psychology behind jealous mothers is complex and deeply rooted in their own unresolved issues and insecurities. As we touched on earlier, narcissistic mothers often see their daughters as extensions of themselves, and when their daughters surpass them in any aspect of life, they feel threatened and envious. This jealousy can manifest in various ways, such as constant criticism, belittling, or even sabotaging their daughters' successes.

Body image is another area where the impact of a narcissistic mother can be devastating for their daughters. They may internalize their mother's critiques of their appearance, leading to a negative body image and even eating disorders. They may feel that they are never good enough, never thin enough, or never beautiful enough to meet their mother's impossible standards.

The influence of a narcissistic mother can also be seen in their daughters' relationships with food. Daughters may develop unhealthy eating habits, such as emotional eating or restrictive dieting, as a way to cope with the stress and anxiety caused by their mother's constant criticism and control.

Academic performance is yet another area where daughters of narcissistic mothers may struggle. They may feel immense pressure to succeed in school, as their mother's love and approval may be contingent on their grades and achievements. This can lead to perfectionism, anxiety, and even self-sabotage, as daughters may feel that they can never live up to their mother's expectations.

The Green-Eyed Mother: When Daughters Dare to Shine

For narcissistic mothers, a daughter's success becomes a personal affront—a direct challenge to their position as the family's central figure. This jealousy intensifies when their daughter begins to surpass them in areas they consider crucial to their own identity: physical appearance, romantic relationships, financial success, or social status.

A daughter's wedding day, for instance, can become a battleground. Rather than celebrating their daughter's happiness, these mothers often try to steal the spotlight or sabotage the event. They might criticize the bride's dress choice, question the groom's suitability, or create drama with the in-laws. The prospect of their daughter joining another family—especially a more affluent or socially connected one—threatens their dominance.

This jealousy extends beyond special occasions. When a daughter develops a close relationship with her in-laws, particularly her mother-in-law, a narcissistic mother often responds with attempts to undermine these bonds. She might spread rumors, manufacture conflicts, or guilt-trip her daughter about "choosing them over family." The fear of being replaced or outshone by another maternal figure drives her to isolate her daughter from these new, potentially nurturing relationships.

Financial success can be particularly triggering. If a daughter achieves greater financial stability than her mother—whether through her own career or marriage—the mother's reaction can be visceral. She might downplay her daughter's achievements, make snide remarks about "selling out," or even attempt to create financial dependence through guilt or manipulation. The daughter's ability to afford a better lifestyle, home, or experiences becomes a source of bitter resentment rather than maternal pride.

Body image and physical appearance form another battleground. A narcissistic mother might have subtle but cutting remarks about her daughter's weight, criticize her fashion choices, or make backhanded compliments about how "brave" she is to wear certain outfits. If the daughter maintains a fit physique or receives positive attention for her appearance, the mother might try to compete or diminish her daughter's confidence through constant criticism.

The mother's jealousy can even extend to her daughter's parenting. When a daughter develops a loving, healthy relationship with her own children, it holds up a mirror to the mother's own failings. Rather than supporting her daughter's parenting journey, she might undermine her decisions, criticize her methods, or try to turn her grandchildren against their mother, recreating the same toxic dynamic with a new generation.

I adored my mom and loved her dearly, despite her flaws. She was like a bad drug that I couldn't stop taking. I believed that she loved me, but that her love was misguided. I thought that maybe one day I would be strong enough to handle her, to calm her stormy waters, or that she would soften as she got older and her demons would go quiet.

I couldn't quite understand why she wasn't able to adore me in a simple, uncomplicated way. I was a high achiever at school, was the Head School Prefect, held many leadership positions, and excelled academically, but nothing was up to her standard. She liked telling everyone about my achievements and that I was going to study law, as she thought it made her look fantastic. But behind the scenes, she was never tender.

During my final year at school, while balancing my high school leadership role and academics, she would regularly leave me for the whole weekend, in a one-bed apartment without a mobile phone, and spend it with her boyfriend. I managed my exams and my own safety while sleeping in that apartment on my own, without a mom who actually cared about how far I got while studying or if I needed any hugs or hot cups of tea.

My drive and ambition weren't the result of her being a supportive mentor. It was all my own fighting spirit—the same spirit she had tried to squash since my childhood. She wasn't my cheerleader and in fact complained about having to drop me off at school for meetings. She wasn't an observant mother and didn't notice I was losing weight before her eyes, even though my friends and my boyfriend Mark's family did. Mark's sister, Abigail, even took me aside one day and tenderly asked if I was okay, suggesting that my weight loss and commitments at school might be taking a toll on me.

The mind games that jealous mothers play can have a profound impact on their daughters' psyches. Daughters may internalize the negative messages they receive from their mothers, leading to a distorted sense of self and a constant need for validation. These beliefs can become so deeply ingrained that they become part of the daughter's subconscious mind, influencing her thoughts, emotions, and behaviors well into adulthood.

Even as a mature woman, when I was studying law and completed my international conversions overseas, my mother never acknowledged my accomplishments. Instead, she would always praise my husband's business and tell him how wonderful he was to put up with me, saying that I was "a lot." Even in my mid-30s, while holding my own babies, I still craved my mother's approval. I thought, *Just say something, mom.*

Looking back, I should have left her earlier. I wouldn't tolerate anyone making snide remarks like that about me now because I know the truth about my worth. And no one messes with my truth.

As daughters of narcissistic mothers navigate the challenges of growing up and forming their own identities, it is crucial that they recognize the impact of their mother's behavior and work toward healing and self-acceptance. This may involve seeking therapy, building supportive relationships, and learning to set healthy boundaries with their mothers.

By sharing my own experiences and insights, I hope to shed light on the complex dynamics of narcissistic motherhood and offer support and validation to those who have faced similar struggles. It is never too late to break free from the cycle of guilt, shame, and control and to embrace your true self with compassion and self-love.

Chapter 6:

Oh No You Don't

Growing up with a narcissistic mother is like being trapped in an endless cycle of trying to please someone who can never be satisfied. Normal parents love unconditionally. Narcissistic mothers, however, are conditional. Their children must comply with their conditions and terms, or else they face the consequences of their mother's bullying and manipulation.

Your Body, Your Mind: The Only Home You'll Ever Have

Before we dive into the toxic contracts of narcissistic motherhood, there's something fundamental you need to understand: Your body and mind are the only vessels you'll ever have in this life. Just as you wouldn't feed a precious plant with poison or deprive it of sunlight, you must be mindful of what you allow to take root in your psyche. The harsh words, the criticism, the self-doubt—these are all toxins that can poison your inner garden.

Children of narcissistic mothers are rarely allowed this basic understanding of self-care and self-preservation. Instead, they're treated more like show ponies than human beings: groomed, trained, and displayed for their mother's benefit. There's no room for individual personality or autonomous development. These children exist primarily as extensions of their mother—living trophies to be paraded before an audience.

I remember a moment that crystallized this truth for me. I was at a dinner party before I'd had my own children, and I overheard two mothers discussing their sons. One asked the other, "So, what is he like? Tell me about his personality." The genuine interest in her voice stopped me in my tracks. These mothers were sharing stories about their children as unique individuals, delighting in their quirks and characteristics.

The conversation stunned me because it revealed what I'd been denied my entire life: the luxury of being seen as a person in my own right. To my mother, I was never "Louise, the girl who loves playing in the garden and eating Black Forest cake, and who has dreams of opening an animal shelter." I was simply her biological daughter, an extension of herself, a being to be molded and controlled rather than understood and nurtured. She never asked about my favorite foods, never shared those intimate mother–daughter moments like playing with my hair or letting me play with hers. The basic building blocks of maternal connection—knowing your child's joys, their comfort foods, their dreams—were missing. She was so disconnected from who I truly was that she had to secretly read my journals to discover my inner world. She never took the time to learn my deepest hopes or fears through genuine conversation and care. Her parenting was mechanical, focused on maintaining control rather than fostering growth.

This mechanical approach to parenting is common among narcissistic mothers. They're not truly invested in their children's best interests or individual development. Instead, they view their children as assets to be managed, trained, and deployed for their own benefit. The child's role is to reflect well on the mother, to achieve what she dictates, and to maintain her preferred image—regardless of their own desires or needs.

I loved studying contract law because, despite the inherent uncertainty in every contractual conflict, if you had an ironclad contract that was agreed upon and signed at the start, applying the principles of contract law was straightforward. You just followed the legislation, applied the precedent from the relevant case, and you could enforce the terms.

In a way, my mother was like a contract. She had emotional contracts with each of us and, as children, we picked sides. We either complied and signed on the dotted line, vowing to be forever grateful and indebted to this glorious woman who had birthed us and sacrificed her whole life for us, or we defaulted and put in an application to rescind or amend our contract with her.

The latter was not actually an option for my nervous or devoted siblings. If you chose it, it was the start of our mother becoming not just a thorn in your side but a sharp metal rod that ran through the top of your brain right down into your feet. Throughout my "former life" as her daughter, I often challenged my mother's "laws" and opinions. She did not want us to challenge her or question her care of us, her parenting, her drinking, or her choice of boyfriends. Criticism was not tolerated. Expressing a desire to visit or live with my father or spend time with other female mentors like my aunt was met with resistance.

As adults, we were expected to manage our mother by not speaking to her as much, but we were also expected to answer her phone calls and not keep any family secrets from her. Family secrets were out. No one had privacy. This lack of boundaries and respect for individual autonomy is a hallmark of narcissistic parenting.

One particularly disturbing incident involved one of my siblings who was molested by a stranger in early childhood. My mother's handling of this was disgusting. My sweet precious sibling was four years old at the time, and after they entrusted our mom with this experience, she announced it at the dinner table, telling all of us what had happened. My mother did not allow for any family secrets. In her eyes, we were a family unit, and no one was allowed to hide anything—not even their trauma. This particular incident in my sibling's life has plagued them ever since. They said that the actual act of the perpetrator was something they could "work through" in time, but my mother's exposure of the incident at the dinner table, her lack of tenderness, and her revolting minimization of the incident is what they found the most damaging.

This type of behavior is not uncommon among narcissistic mothers. They often deny and minimize their children's truths, gaslighting them and making them question their own perceptions and memories of events. If a child tries to express their feelings of hurt or neglect, their narcissistic mother may dismiss those feelings, telling the child that they are too sensitive or that they are misinterpreting the situation.

Overall, my mother expected us to share details about our relationships with our spouses and make time to see her. She had to be a priority unless we had a good reason, like having just given birth and being a bit busy. My mother viewed herself as almost holy. She was "the divine."

We were required to apologize to her whenever we "messed up," but, dear Lord, we would never get an apology back.

Narcissistic mothers may also use guilt and emotional blackmail to keep their children in line. They will often remind their children of all the sacrifices they have made for them, making the children feel indebted and obligated to comply with their mother's wishes. If a child tries to set boundaries or assert their independence, a narcissistic mother may react with anger, tears, or accusations of abandonment, manipulating the child into staying under their control.

In addition to these behaviors, narcissistic mothers tend to be be highly critical of their children, constantly finding fault with their appearance, their choices, or their accomplishments. You may well recognize the feeling: No matter how hard you try, you never feel good enough or worthy of your mother's love and approval. These mothers may also ignore or dismiss their children's emotional needs, use them as pawns in their own conflicts, invade their privacy, sabotage their relationships or successes, and play favorites among their children.

As I know only too well from my own family, growing up with a narcissistic mother can leave deep and long-lasting emotional scars. Conditional parenting, a hallmark of narcissistic mothers, can have profound effects on children that extend well into their adult lives. In this type of parenting, a child's experience of love and acceptance is contingent upon meeting their mother's often unrealistic expectations and demands. As a result, they internalize the message that they are not worthy of love simply for who they are, but rather that receiving love depends on what they do or how well they comply with their mother's wishes.

Conditional parenting can create a deep sense of insecurity and self-doubt in children. They may constantly question their own worth and feel that they must earn love and approval through their actions and achievements. This can lead to a pattern of people-pleasing, where the child suppresses their own needs and desires in order to gain acceptance from others.

The effects of this parenting style can be seen in various areas of a child's life, even as they grow into adulthood. In their relationships, they may struggle with intimacy and trust, always fearing that their partner's love is conditional and that they will be rejected if they don't meet certain expectations. They may also have difficulty setting healthy boundaries, as they have been taught that their own needs are secondary to those of others.

In their professional lives, children of narcissistic mothers may be driven to achieve and succeed, but never feel satisfied with their accomplishments. They may be perfectionists, setting impossibly high standards for themselves and feeling like failures if they do not meet them. They may also struggle with authority figures, either fearing criticism and disapproval or rebelling against any form of control.

This was certainly true for me. After navigating life from childhood through adolescence and into adulthood, I realized there was another enemy in my midst. It wasn't my boss, a sibling, or my husband's ex-wife. It was me. I was my own enemy because I was self-sabotaging. Deep down, I didn't like myself and I didn't think I was worthy. Deep down, I was ashamed of who I was. I had all the accolades to prove my intelligence, and I was told I excelled at my job. Every opportunity I wanted, I got.

I pushed myself relentlessly in everything. It had to be perfect, whether it was my home décor, the quality of my breast milk, my fashion choices, or my son's zombie graveyard birthday cake! I had to look the part as well as play the part. I was a skilled actress in my own life. It's a wonder I never became seriously ill, because I often exhausted myself to tears. In reality, I doubted myself, lacked strong boundaries, and didn't know who I was. I knew who I wanted to be from a very young age. I used to cut pictures out of magazines and create what I now realize were manifestation boards. I would escape into my head and imagine what my life would look like as an adult, how I would feel inside. I knew what I wanted, but I didn't know how to get it.

Healing from the effects of conditional parenting is a gradual and often challenging process. It requires unlearning the toxic messages that you've internalized and replacing them with healthier, more self-affirming beliefs. It involves learning to validate your own emotions and experiences, developing a sense of self-compassion and self-acceptance, and treating yourself with the same empathy and care that you would extend to a good friend.

The key to healing is healing yourself and befriending yourself. Forgive yourself for all the times you thought you messed up. Maybe you did. The most important thing with those life mess-ups is realizing why they happened, apologizing if necessary, and including yourself in that apology.

As a child, you were fractured at a very young age, and were told that whatever and whoever you were was wrong and needed to change. You needed to be "tweaked." So, the key is to relearn who you are and where you want to be in the future. Ask yourself these simple questions: Who am I? Who do I want to be? What do I want my life to look like? How do I want to feel about myself and my life?

Some of you might have no clue who you are. Don't panic; I didn't either. You might also feel rudderless. Everyone might think you have it all together, but inside you are so mashed up. It's important to first clear out the emotional beliefs you have about yourself. Once you've wiped the slate clean, you can focus on who you want to be. Who is that girl? What is she?

Growing up with a person who makes you doubt your own sanity and judgment is like a tree trying to grow with mangled roots. It's not going to get far. But with time, patience, and a commitment to self-discovery and self-care, it is possible to heal your wounds and flourish into the person you were always meant to be.

Chapter 7:

"Stroke, Stroke, Slap"

Abuse grows from attitudes and values, not feelings. The roots are ownership, the trunk is entitlement, and the branches are control. –Lundy Bancroft

Relationships between narcissistic mothers and their children are inherently abusive, operating on the same principles of power, control, and intermittent reinforcement that characterize other forms of domestic abuse. Just as an abusive spouse might follow a violent outburst with apologies and gifts, a narcissistic parent punctuates their cruelty with occasional warmth. This inconsistency is deeply destabilizing, keeping the victim trapped in a cycle of hope and disappointment.

In mediation training, we are taught a strategy of "stroke, stroke, slap." What this means is that when we are dealing with a high-conflict party, we stroke softly on a point of contention, then stroke again, softening them slightly; then, we go in strong with a good verbal "slap" that asserts serious boundaries.

At the core of these dynamics is an imbalance of power. The abuser, feeling entitled to dominance, employs various tactics to maintain control. This can range from overt intimidation like yelling and threats to more insidious forms like gaslighting, silent treatment, and withholding affection. The goal is always to undermine the victim's autonomy and keep them compliant.

In parent–child relationships, this power differential is pronounced, as children are inherently dependent on their caregivers. A narcissistic mother exploits this vulnerability, wielding her influence to demand subservience and punish independence. Her love becomes contingent on how well her child meets her needs.

This was the painful reality of my own upbringing. My mother could be doting one moment and dismissive the next. She'd shower me with affection when I made her look good, then turn cold when I expressed needs of my own. Her regard always felt precarious, like it could be revoked at any misstep.

Narcissistic mothers are masters at presenting a loving facade that conceals their true self-absorption. They skillfully feign devotion and claim their controlling behaviors are for your own good. But scratch the surface and you'll find a staggering lack of empathy, even toward their own children.

The Consequences of Conditional Love

Growing up in this environment of conditional love is profoundly damaging. You learn that your worth is tied to your performance, your ability to please and appease. Any authentic expression of self is a risk, as it may shatter the illusion of perfection your mother demands. So, you become a chameleon, morphing yourself to fit her ever-shifting expectations.

But it's a losing game. No matter how hard you try, you can never fully embody her ideal. The goalposts always move, leaving you perpetually striving but always falling short. This seeds a deep sense of defectiveness, a belief that you're fundamentally flawed and unlovable. If your own mother can't love you unconditionally, who could?

This corrosive shame takes root early and burrows deep. It colors every subsequent relationship, as you unconsciously seek out the same conditional love, believing it's all you deserve. You become hypervigilant to others' reactions, constantly scanning for signs of disapproval or withdrawal. The slightest hint of coldness can send you into a spiral of self-recrimination and frantic efforts to repair the rupture.

My mother exemplified this lack of attunement in her treatment of our family pets. She had a habit of adopting adorable white Maltese puppies, only to rehome them when they became too burdensome. Maintaining a pristine house was more important to her than honoring the bond between a child and their dog.

I was particularly devastated when at the age of 13, after my parents' divorce, we had to give up my two beloved dogs because we were moving to a pet-free apartment. My two dogs were gorgeous crossbreeds of Staffordshire Bull Terrier and Ridgeback. I spent hours with them every day, alone in our garden. Those dogs were my friends.

Initially, my father kindly housed them for as long as he could, knowing how much they meant to me. But eventually, he too had to relocate. One of the hardest moments of my life was walking into the animal shelter with my dad and physically surrendering my two best friends. I remember, in between my tears falling, taking their collars off before they were taken away. I kept them as a memory, so I could at least smell them when I missed my dogs. I walked out of that shelter 10 years older than when I had walked in. My heart had broken.

I phoned the shelter a few weeks later to ask if the dogs had been adopted and if my request for them to be rehomed together had at least been granted. I could sense that the lady felt my pain and placated me regardless of the truth.

But from my mother, I received no empathy—not even a hug or a kind word acknowledging my grief. And I was grieving. For the loss of my parents' marriage and for my dog friends. She was impatient with my tears, seeing them as an overreaction to the loss of "just dogs." There was no attempt to comfort me or help me process the heartbreak. I was expected to swallow my pain and carry on.

This theme of dismissing my feelings would persist throughout my life. No matter my accomplishments or milestones, that 13-year-old girl remained lodged within, aching for the tenderness that I never received. It wasn't until well into my 30s, through intensive therapy, that I could begin to unpack the impact of that pivotal moment and a lifetime of similar emotional neglect.

This lack of attunement is insidious and wildly damaging to a child's developing psyche. We learn about our worth and how to handle big feelings through mirroring our parents. When our distress is routinely minimized or punished, we absorb the lesson that our emotions are shameful burdens. We become alienated from our own inner worlds, never learning how to self-regulate or self-soothe.

Living in this constant state of emotional deprivation and anxiety breeds a profound disconnection from self. When our authentic feelings and needs are continuously undermined, we lose touch with our own inner compass. We become reliant on others for validation and direction, as we've never learned to trust our own instincts.

This leaves us vulnerable to further abuse and exploitation, as we've been conditioned to override our own discomfort for others' comfort. We may find yourself in one-sided, depleting relationships that echo the dynamics between ourselves and our mother. Or we may isolate ourselves entirely, believing we're too damaged to be loved.

The Trauma of Intermittent Reinforcement

But perhaps most disorienting is how a narcissistic mother's coldness will be interspersed with occasional warmth. Desperate for her approval, we cling to those glimmers of affection, convincing ourselves they reflect her true feelings. In this way, the harsher treatment becomes easy to rationalize: If only we work harder to please her, we'll get the consistent love we crave.

It's the ultimate setup, of course, as it's impossible to earn what should be freely given. But traumatic bonds run deep, and walking away feels unbearable when we're enmeshed in the dysfunction. We're biologically driven to seek our mother's love, so losing even a toxic connection can feel life-threatening. Our nervous systems become addicted to the intermittent rewards, holding out for those elusive reprieves from the tension.

This is the insidious trap of trauma bonding. Abuse and affection become so intertwined that we start to associate love with pain. The intense push–pull of the relationship becomes addictive, as our brains are flooded with dopamine during the fleeting moments of connection. We become hooked on the drama, mistaking the intensity for intimacy.

Breaking free from this cycle is incredibly difficult. It requires facing the heartbreaking reality that the love we so desperately crave will never come, no matter how hard we try. We have to grieve the mother we needed but never had and learn to give ourselves the nurturing she couldn't provide. It's a long, arduous journey of untangling our sense of worth from our mother's approval.

"The Two Wolves": A Cherokee Story

A young boy came to his grandfather, filled with anger at another boy who had done him an injustice. The old grandfather said to his grandson, "Let me tell you a story. I too, at times, have felt a great hate for those who have taken so much with no sorrow for what they have done. But hate wears you down, and hate does not hurt your enemy. Hate is like taking poison and wishing your enemy would die. I have struggled with these feelings many times.

"It is as if there are two wolves inside me. One wolf is good and does no harm. He lives in harmony with all around him and does not take offense when no offense was intended. He will only fight when it is right to do so, and in the right way. But the other wolf is full of anger. The littlest thing will set him into a fit of temper.

"He fights everyone, all the time, for no reason. He cannot think because his anger and hate are so great. It is helpless anger, because his anger will change nothing. Sometimes it is hard to live with these two wolves inside me, because both of the wolves try to dominate my spirit."

The boy looked intently into his grandfather's eyes and asked, "Which wolf will win, Grandfather?"

The grandfather smiled and said, "The one I feed."

This analogy is one that has stuck with me through the years. I firmly believe in the power of the mind. Once you have cleared out your old, untrue self-beliefs (be it on your own or with the guidance of a professional), you will then need to work very hard at keeping your mind unpolluted and preventing those old beliefs and patterns from taking root again.

You are what you believe. You have to be careful when you give in to negative thoughts about yourself and shy away from promotions or new relationships. Sometimes, our feelings of doubt or self-loathing are too familiar to us because we've had them for so long; as a result, we can wallow in them, leading to self-pity and stagnation. You have to decide what you want to believe and feed the right wolf!

It's like training for a marathon. Relearning your self-beliefs is not easy, but it's possible. Just like athletes and academics work hard at their craft and get up early to train or do more research, you too have to keep on working hard and practicing new positive lifestyle changes and self-beliefs. This is now a training of the mind. You are changing your life completely, for the better.

You are going to become the woman you always wanted to be.

The journey from surviving to thriving after narcissistic abuse is not a linear one. There will be days when the old hooks of shame and self-doubt resurface, tempting you to fall back into familiar patterns. Healing requires vigilance and a commitment to choosing yourself even when it feels foreign and scary.

This self-love is the antidote to the poison of narcissistic abuse. It is the salve that heals the deepest wounds, the light that illuminates the darkest corners of shame. It is the foundation upon which you will build a life of authentic joy and connection, a life that honors your true self in all its imperfect beauty.

Chapter 8:

Deflated Balloon

Children learn what they live. –Dorothy Law Nolte

Our childhood experiences shape us in profound and lasting ways. The messages we receive from our caregivers, both verbal and nonverbal, form the bedrock of our self-concept. When those messages are affirming and nurturing, we develop a sturdy sense of worth that carries us through life's challenges. But when they are critical, dismissive, or inconsistent, the very foundation of our being becomes shaky and unstable.

I've always been drawn to the famous poem—which hung in my childhood home, ironically—by Dorothy Law Nolte titled "Children Learn What They Live." It's a simple yet profound piece that encapsulates the idea that no matter what you think you are teaching your children, they are learning from what they experience in their lives. They base their learning upon their perceptions. For example, if a child lives with criticism, they learn to condemn. If a child lives with hostility, they learn to fight. On the other hand, if a child lives with tolerance, they learn to be patient. If a child lives with encouragement, they learn confidence.

Growing up with a narcissistic mother, I experienced firsthand how toxic messages can erode a child's sense of self. My mother was a master at instilling shame and self-doubt, chipping away at my self-esteem until I felt like a mere shadow of my potential. Like a balloon losing air, my sense of self became smaller and smaller until I was left feeling utterly deflated.

At the core of this deflation lay shame, the belief that I was inherently flawed and unworthy of love. My mother bred this shame in a myriad of ways, from overt criticism to subtle jabs disguised as jokes. She would mock my appearance, belittle my accomplishments, and compare me unfavorably to others. Over time, I internalized these messages, coming to see myself as fundamentally defective.

Looking back, I realize that children whose childhood environments don't nurture but instead criticize are like balloons that get blown up and then deflated at their mother's whim. We are filled with potential and life, only to have it repeatedly squeezed out of us by the very person who should be supporting and encouraging us.

Guilt was another potent weapon in my mother's arsenal. By constantly blaming and guilting me for her own shortcomings, she offloaded responsibility and kept the focus on my perceived failings. I learned to take on inappropriate levels of responsibility, believing that I was the cause of her unhappiness or our family's dysfunction.

This guilt was often compounded by my mother's unrealistic expectations. She demanded perfection in every arena, setting the bar impossibly high and then berating me for falling short. Academic achievement, athletic prowess, physical appearance—no area was off limits for her scrutiny and judgment.

Desperate for her approval, I drove myself to the brink trying to meet these expectations. I excelled in school, pushed myself in extracurriculars, and strived to maintain an impeccable image. But no matter my achievements, it was never enough. The finish line was always moved, the carrot dangling just out of reach. As I grew up, I became a self-critical adult who could be extremely hard on myself, perpetuating the mistruths that my mother had originally taught me.

Even more insidious was how my mother squashed my individual dreams and desires. She had a specific vision for my life, one that reflected well on her and satisfied her own unmet needs. Whether it was pressure to follow a certain career path, attend a particular school, or even marry a specific type of person, the message was clear: What I wanted didn't matter. My sole purpose was to fulfill her agenda.

Any deviation from this path was met with guilt, shaming, and emotional blackmail. My unique passions and inclinations became sources of disappointment or embarrassment for my mother, something to be stifled and hidden away. Slowly, I learned to dissociate from my own desires, to see them as shameful or selfish. I became disconnected from my authentic self and a mere extension of my mother's ego.

This bred a profound sense of inauthenticity, a feeling of being an imposter in my own life. I learned to perform, to mold myself into whatever shape pleased my mother. I became an expert chameleon, adept at reading the room and adjusting accordingly. But this came at a steep price: a gnawing sense of emptiness and a pervasive feeling that something was missing.

I remember catching glimpses of myself in the bathroom mirror after pulling my kids out of the bath. As I was holding them up to the mirror and laughing with them all wrapped up in their snuggly towels, their hair wet, I would sometimes, briefly, look at myself. In those moments, I was often embarrassed—I looked so tired and worn out. Other times, I thought to myself, *Who the fuck is that? Who is she really?*

This sense of disconnection from my true self is a common experience for adult children of narcissistic mothers. The constant pressure to conform to our mother's expectations and the lack of validation for our own desires can lead to a profound sense of emptiness and inauthenticity that persists well into adulthood.

It's a painful realization, but one that is necessary for healing and growth. By acknowledging the impact of our childhood experiences and the toxic messages we received, we can begin to reclaim our true selves. We can learn to validate our own desires, to pursue our passions without guilt or shame, and to build a life that is authentic and fulfilling.

It's a journey that requires courage, self-compassion, and a willingness to confront the painful truths of our past. But it's a journey worth taking, for it leads us back to ourselves, to the vibrant, resilient beings we were always meant to be. As we heal and grow, we can break the cycle of narcissistic abuse and create a new legacy for ourselves and our children—one of love, acceptance, and true authenticity.

Finding Sanctuary in Imagination

For some children of narcissistic mothers, imagination becomes a lifeline. They create rich inner worlds where they can retreat from the constant judgment and chaos. Whether it's through art, writing, music, or simply daydreaming, they find solace in these private sanctuaries.

As these children grow into adults, the impact of their narcissistic upbringing continues to shape their inner world. The coping mechanisms they developed in childhood, such as escapism into imagination, may no longer serve them in the same way. They may find themselves struggling with a deep sense of emptiness, feeling disconnected from their authentic desires and passions. The constant pressure to conform to their mother's expectations can lead to a profound sense of inauthenticity, leaving them feeling like imposters in their own lives.

For example, an adult child of a narcissistic mother may pursue a career path that aligns with their mother's wishes but leaves them feeling unfulfilled and drained. They may find themselves in relationships that mirror the toxic dynamics of their childhood, constantly seeking approval and validation from emotionally unavailable partners. The inner critic, shaped by years of maternal criticism, may continue to undermine their self-worth and autonomy.

This was certainly true for me. From a young age, I escaped into my room, playing with my dolls' house for hours on end. I would also retreat to the garden to play and talk to my beloved dogs. I spent hours in the garden, literally. Lost in a magical and safe world in my head.

Of course, this innocent escape was not to my mother's liking either. She labeled me as odd, questioning why I sat in the garden for so long, lost in my own world. My siblings, taking their cue from her, would also comment on my behavior. She would openly discuss with her friends, in front of me, how I needed to see a psychologist. Gradually, I internalized the belief that I was different, that something was wrong with me.

But deep down, in my resilient spirit, in my survival backpack, I knew that my difference was a strength, not a weakness. I understood, even then, why I retreated to the garden, to my dolls, to my imagination. It was a form of escapism, a way to protect my true self from the constant onslaught of criticism and judgment.

My mother, like many narcissistic parents, had a way of turning the simplest things, the things she didn't understand, into weapons. My love for the outdoors, my rich imaginative play—these were not signs of dysfunction, but marks of a brilliant, creative child. But in her narrative, they became evidence of my oddness, my defectiveness.

If you too grew up with a narcissistic mother, you may be all too familiar with this experience of being gradually deflated. You may have internalized toxic shame, guilt, and self-doubt, feeling like a pale imitation of who you could be.

The first step is to recognize that the beliefs instilled by your mother are not truths but lies born from her own dysfunction. You are not flawed, selfish, or unlovable. You are a unique individual with inherent worth, deserving of love, respect, and autonomy. Your desires, passions, and boundaries are valid and valuable, no matter how much they may have been dismissed or trampled.

My greatest gift and power is that I really like and love myself. I never used to. I wanted to, but I didn't really understand this "self-love" concept. My mother didn't model self-love for herself, so, coupled with the fact that I felt awful about myself, it was new territory for me to navigate. I didn't really know myself either.

Nowadays, I know all about me, and no one can knock me from my perch. I sit there proudly. I don't mind at all catching glimpses of myself in the mirror. I'm so proud of myself, flaws and all. I wear my bikini on whatever beach I'm on, and I've mastered a two-minute makeup routine followed by a spritz of my Tom Ford perfume as I race out the door.

Although I've been told I'm a good attorney, I realize my personality doesn't suit a work environment focused on solving conflict; I prefer the academic environment, where I can be with students from all walks of life and ages. I accept that I am clumsy with my hands, so blow-drying my hair to perfection like Kate Middleton is not my gift—but explaining legal concepts to a class of students and cooking the perfect rare steak for my family is!

I don't make excuses for the fact that I'm not particularly social and would prefer to be at home tucked up in bed by 8 p.m. watching something on my iPad, or staying up past midnight pruning my plants because something caught my attention on one of the leaves. I decline whatever "too big" event invitations I receive because I know I thrive on one-on-one company. I know I need nature, and living in the city 24/7 means I need an easy out to my favorite destinations close by.

I can spot someone who beeps on my radar as a "toxic" tick from my past or someone who is lost, draining, and craving my energy and stability. I can feel my body and energy change around those people, and I adjust accordingly. I happily assert my boundaries with anyone— except my dogs, who still have their way of softening me.

I softly forgive myself, and when I think of the old "cringe" chaotic decisions I made in the past, I know that I'm human and that I am not chained to my past. What matters is the now, that I have corrected my coping strategies, and that life is about beautiful learning. I'm thankful to life for enriching me with these opportunities for learning and that, thank fuck, I passed those old lessons and moved on!

Rising From the Ashes

As you begin to shed the false layers and limitations imposed by your mother, you may find a profound resilience emerging. Like a phoenix rising from the ashes, you are reborn, stronger, wiser, and more authentic. Your past wounds become sources of empathy, fueling your ability to connect with others on a deep level. Your hard-won self-knowledge becomes a compass, guiding you toward a life of meaning and fulfillment.

In this rebirth, you may even find a new appreciation for the very qualities your mother disparaged: your sensitivity, your creativity, your nonconformity. These are not weaknesses but superpowers. They enable you to see the world through a unique lens, to find beauty and meaning where others overlook it. They are the keys to your own personal liberation.

However, it's not enough just to realize where all your wounds have come from and work on a plan to deal with or break up with your abuser. You actually have to decide to break ties with the old version of yourself. Like a balloon, flowing off peacefully into the air, you have to let your old self go. This means shedding the layers of shame, guilt, and self-doubt that have weighed you down for so long. It means embracing your true self, the self that has always been there beneath the scars and the masks.

The truth has always been within you: You were born complete, carrying every strength and resource you would ever need. It was the world—and especially your mother's distorted lens—that made you doubt this innate wholeness. You have always been enough, exactly as you are. The feelings of inadequacy were learned, not innate; they were imposed, not inherent.

So, to all the deflated daughters out there, know that your story doesn't end here. You have the power to rewrite the narrative, to define yourself on your own terms. Your mother may have taught you that you were too much or never enough, but the truth is, you are exactly as you should be. Messy, complex, brilliant, evolving—and utterly worthy of love.

There will be days when your true nature emerges fierce and untamed, and that's something to celebrate, not apologize for. Those parts of yourself that don't conform to others' expectations? They're not flaws to be corrected—they're the very essence of your authentic self. This raw, uncontained spirit within you is your power source, your wellspring of strength. It refuses to be diminished by anyone's judgment or confined by their limitations.

So, embrace your inner wolf, your fierce and untamed spirit. Allow yourself to be fully expressed, unapologetically you. In a world that often demands conformity, your wildness is a revolutionary act of self-love and reclamation. Howl your truth, run free through the forests of your imagination, and trust that your path, no matter how winding or unconventional, is leading you exactly where you need to go.

Chapter 9:

Bullet Holes

Stop trying to calm the storm. Calm yourself. The storm will pass. –Buddha

Trauma can take many forms. It's not just the result of physical abuse or violence, but also the more insidious emotional and psychological wounds inflicted by coercive control, verbal threats, lies, and manipulation. These are especially damaging when they come from a parent or primary caregiver during a child's critical early development.

We know that children in domestically violent families are scarred not only by physical beatings but by also the ongoing abuse of coercive control (Katz, 2016). Historically, psychological damage to children was measured primarily by the Physical Incident Model, which focuses on specific, significant acts of violence. However, the behaviors that make up coercive control, such as isolation from family and friends, monitoring, and verbal, psychological, or emotional abuse, can be just as damaging. Victims have reported that a verbal threat can be as frightening and harmful as a physical blow.

The scars from a narcissistic mother's poisonous lies, veiled threats, and disguised insults, repeatedly inflicted over years from childhood into adulthood, are like bullet holes. They penetrate deep into your psyche, your sense of self. It's an insidious form of brainwashing that only the strong and emotionally intelligent can fully unpack and heal from. Many, like my siblings, stay with the dysfunction because facing and processing that pain requires immense effort.

It's like the analogy of a frog in water: If thrown into boiling water, it will immediately jump out. But if put in cold water that is slowly brought to a boil, it doesn't notice the gradual temperature change and is cooked alive. Emotional abuse from a narcissistic mother is similar. It begins in childhood and slowly ramps up in intensity over time. As a child or teen, you can't understand why you feel so displaced in your own body and so confused in your beliefs about yourself.

A critical aspect of childhood development is forming a healthy self-image and self-esteem. The messages absorbed from our parents become the foundation of our identity. In my case, my mother constantly disparaged her own body, especially her legs. She read me a storybook about an air hostess, pointing out the "big legs" in the illustrations and telling me I had legs just like that, just like hers.

The meaning I internalized was clear: Mom hates her body, and she says mine looks like hers; therefore, my body is unacceptable and ugly too. That seed, planted so young, grew into a deeply negative body image that plagued me for decades. In my teens, I developed an eating disorder, a secret struggle my mother dismissed, minimized, and gossiped about rather than compassionately supporting me through it. Then, in my adult years, I turned to food as a comfort and was overweight due to unhealthy emotional eating.

It wasn't until my mid-30s, after separating from my mother, that I finally cleared out those toxic emotional wounds and beliefs. I lost weight but, more importantly, I learned to love my body and myself unconditionally. I proudly wear a bikini now because I've changed how I view myself. But it took a lot of work to get here.

I thank my body, especially my beautiful legs, for being so strong. I have run a few races with these gorgeous legs, and they have helped me carry my children on my hips, move boxes between various homes, and dance at my wedding—as well as at random times in my kitchen when a good song comes on! There was nothing ever "wrong" with my body. It was never fat, nor thin, nor did it need to be changed. It just fucking was as it needed to be. And now I love it.

Had I not changed my life and loved myself, I would still be wearing long shorts at the beach and to go swimming in Fiji with my kids, and avoiding playing with my nieces in the sand at the beach in front of my siblings. Lies that are told in childhood are crippling. It is imperative to change them.

Various Methods of Therapy

In the previous chapters, I discussed how to recognize your mother's toxic behavior and educate yourself by reading and understanding how these mothers distort your reality and beliefs about yourself from a young age. I hope it has reaffirmed that what you've been feeling all these years is not imaginary or some undiagnosed mental health problem! Now that you have this knowledge, it is important to take action and make a commitment to healing and becoming a new version of yourself.

Healing from childhood trauma and reshaping your identity is a deeply personal journey. What helps one person may not work for another. The most important thing is finding tools and support to bring you self-understanding and peace.

Traditional talk therapy modalities like cognitive behavioral therapy (CBT) can help identify and change unhealthy thought patterns and behaviors. Eye movement desensitization and reprocessing (EMDR) is an evidence-based treatment that helps the brain reprocess disturbing memories in a healthier way. Psychodynamic therapy delves into childhood experiences and unconscious mental processes.

Some find healing through body-based and experiential methods. Somatic experiencing focuses on releasing trauma held in the body. Art therapy, music therapy, and journaling provide creative outlets that can help you express and process emotions. Yoga, meditation, and mindfulness practices can help calm the nervous system and provide a sense of grounding and self-regulation.

In my own journey, I tried it all: psychologists, psychiatrists, psychics, church ministers, yoga, meditation, journaling, and symbolic release rituals like writing and burning letters to those who hurt me. What ultimately helped me most was working with a trauma-informed practitioner. She used a technique involving hypnosis and visualization to rapidly process and release traumas held in my subconscious mind.

At first, my subconscious resisted, as I had become so accustomed to my inner pain and turmoil. But one of the most powerful exercises I did during my healing was identifying stressful moments of my life—not necessarily huge, dramatic events, but the memories that jump out as instances where I felt most scared, ashamed, or guilty. It was healing to look at the moments that I listed. Some were fleeting moments or passing comments, but they had been lodged and stuck within me for so long.

Processing these painful experiences left me feeling not unhinged but unlocked. It was as if gears that had been stuck for so long were finally moving. I felt an openness and lightness, like sunshine pouring into all the dark places inside. I continue to do trauma sessions as needed, while also incorporating other supportive healing practices.

Ultimately, the journey of healing my mind helped heal my body too, and I released 60 pounds of emotional weight I had been carrying for years. Beyond the physical, I gained an unshakable sense of self-worth and self-love.

Rewriting your story and redefining your identity takes immense courage and commitment. But on the other side of that storm is a joy, freedom, and wholeness beyond anything you've ever imagined.

Take your time to find the right modality of healing; you may need a combination of practices, or a few attempts at finding the right practitioner. Once you've gone for emotional "reconstructive surgery" in whatever form, you will feel tender. Healing from any abusive relationship is like being shot by a bazooka. Do not rush your recovery or think that because you have physically left the relationship, you are going to spring back to a wonderful new you. No, my dear; the work is just beginning. Your bravery, your act of self-love by leaving the relationship and recognizing that you deserve better, was the first act. Now the healing comes. Be careful who you associate with and how you exchange your energy with others during this time. Your wound is fresh, and it can get easily infected. Septic.

You will need to put on your big girl panties for this challenge. Just like Bridget Jones whipped on that huge, unsightly, oversized pair, you are going to need to do the same, because this journey of self-love exploration is not for the faint-hearted.

But here's the key: There are two types of people who "survive" something.

The first type bravely does the act, starts the healing work, and then… plateaus out. They remain stuck in the trauma. Licking their childhood wounds, reminding themselves indirectly that they have had these wounds, and using them to define their identity. For example, they proudly wear the badge of "I am the daughter of a narcissistic mother" or "I am a survivor of a toxic mother." Both are true, but it's in the past, so why bring that into who you are today? It's like reminding yourself how bad last month's menstrual period was. You've moved on, found great painkillers, or had a hysterectomy! You don't lament and say that you are a survivor of February's menstrual cycle. You know what your body needs and what has happened in the past, and you know how to deal with it in the future. These healing plateau people are in effect re-traumatizing themselves and staying stuck. Using your past painful experiences should propel you to new heights and new beginnings within yourself. They shouldn't remind you of what you went through or keep you stuck. These survivors don't realize that they are not letting it go.

The second type of survivor recognizes the wrong, corrects the behavior, and learns and establishes new core self-beliefs, but doesn't stay attached to the healed wound. They don't lament. They may get triggered, but they recognize where it's coming from and correct it so it doesn't fester again. They acknowledge that they were wronged, but they use the wrong to their advantage rather than staying stuck in those comfortable, indulgent feelings of "poor me." They move the fuck on and make million-dollar lemonade out of unripened lemons. And they reframe their story.

Remember that survivors are not perfect. I too have my days when something crops up that is reminiscent of my past. After all, we're human—and we are here to learn lessons.

When I'm triggered, I can sense it in my body, in my dreams, in my mood; I start to feel unsteady in my internal footing. I have learned over the years to recognize the signs and I now actively start working on bringing those triggers forward and challenging why I'm feeling that way. I don't push it aside; it's there to tell me that there is still stuff that needs my awareness or that there may be a person in my life who is pushing my boundaries. They might not even be aware of it, but I am. Just as I would take a headache pill straight away for a headache or rest my muscles if they ached, I do the same with an emotional trigger. I actively find the source and treat it with a conscious response.

My teenage daughter has often found old photos of me when she and my son were younger, back when I hadn't yet made peace with myself. She has commented that my eyes in the "happy" photographs look sad. I was taken aback. I thought I looked happy but, on closer inspection, she was right. At the time, I knew I was sad, but I didn't think I was showing it. But your children absorb things and pick up when you are off-kilter. I look back at those photographs and I can see the sadness, the lostness, the barrenness, even though I was trying to be in the moment, or at least I thought I was. I look back at old photos now and I could have been anywhere: back at school at 17 years old, standing there in my blazer at an awards ceremony with my accolades in my hands, looking timid. Or holding my young babies on holiday with my husband, in some lovely ski resort in Switzerland. I was there physically, but in my subconscious, I was somewhere else.

I want to put my arms around my younger self and tell her that her life is going to turn around 180 degrees after the healing. That she is going to get better and explode with goodness and opportunity; that I understand why she was the way she was and why she believed the things she did. She did her best with what she had and what she knew at the time. I would take her under my wing like an older sister. I would look back as her mentor and tell her to be gentle on herself, and that the best is yet to come. And that she has no idea how good it will be!

In the words of Paulo Coelho (n.d.), "Maybe the journey isn't so much about becoming anything. Maybe it's about unbecoming everything that isn't really you, so you can be who you are meant to be in the first place."

Who Are Your "People"?

When you do the healing work, and you commit to your journey of being well, you will need to assess the company you keep.

As humans, we are energetic beings, and each interaction or relationship we have is based on an energy exchange. I'm sure you will have experienced how, with some friends, you walk away from them after a coffee date or holiday and you feel depleted, agitated, angry, or just plain bored. Sometimes you even need a nap!

Then there's the other mob, who are your people. You never want to cancel or postpone a date with them; you feel energized or inspired when you leave them and they accept you—just as you are.

Going forward in your new life, you need to be very clear about who makes your:

- top people list
- acceptable family list
- unacceptable family list
- limited friends list (they are nice and they are accepting of you, they may even adore you, but you can differ on the big stuff)
- "never to repeat" people list (the people on your "never to repeat" list are those who have come into your life to teach a lesson, but that is it; they are toxic, they are damaged goods, and their mere fractured existence will bring you down and keep you from your destiny)

I repeat: You must be very clear about who sits on which list.

I spoke with my beautician recently. I hadn't seen her in a while, and I knew she had been battling for years with her stubborn weight around her tummy. She always looked like she was "searching" and wanted me to talk more about either legal issues surrounding divorce or how I put firm boundaries in place. I knew she was "on a path of learning."

I commented on how fabulous she looked. She had lost that stubborn abdominal weight and her eyes looked "clearer," like she'd had mist lifted from them. We chatted and I asked, "What did you do to bring about this change?" expecting her to tell me she had been on Ozempic!

She replied, "I broke up with my adult daughters."

I laughed out loud while she waxed my eyebrows and said how fantastic that she'd recognized her daughters were toxic and just using her for her money—and that leaving her marriage to their father and finding someone who actually celebrated her was courageous. It had taken guts and bravery to assert such boundaries of self-love after years of being used, gaslit, and manipulated by her own adult daughters. My beautician was finally putting herself and her needs first.

A quote by Karen Salmahnsohn (2016) says that "You will be too much for some people. Those aren't your people." So, who are your people? Think about it.

Only you will know. And surprisingly, most of your family likely won't make it into your top peeps list. So, have a hard think and don't be afraid to be like Santa Claus, who annually updates his naughty and nice list.

Anyone who knows me will be aware that I love nature. When we lived in South Africa, we often used to frequent the various game reserves to go on safari. I used to marvel as I observed the predators, and more specifically the big cats, in their natural environment. The laws of nature can teach you a lot. The lionesses were so fiercely protective over their young. They knew that they had to protect, love, and nurture their young in order for them to eventually survive on their own one day, be it in or out of the pride. Over the years as an adult, when Sylvia was having one of her tiresome episodes of destructive love, I would think about a lioness with her cubs. Lionesses generally don't eat their cubs. They will stand up to male lions to defend their young, but it's against the laws of nature to want to harm their own offspring. So, while I took my own little kids on safari, I pondered why Sylvia would want to turn the rest of the pride against me and devour me until I didn't have much left. On the inside, I felt like a paraplegic cub. I felt that I was emotionally disabled.

Family is ideally supposed to be "your tribe," your people. But let's be honest: Sometimes the enemy comes from within your tribe.

I am very strict when it comes to my boundaries, and nowadays I run with a happy and empowered pride. As I get older, I don't waste my time. It's too valuable and I've worked too hard to tiptoe around people, particularly family, just because they are "family."

For me now, being family does not give you right of access to my life. It may not even get you a ride home from the airport if I feel that your presence and conversation will drain me. That's what Ubers are for. I am also very particular about which guests can stay at my home, and that includes family. I know which people I like but may not gel with for longer than two hours at a time. So, having those people stay in my home and see me in my dressing gown the next morning is possibly going to send me on a vent to my poor husband. I know myself too well. My people know my limits, and I make no excuses.

The ones who challenge my boundaries and push them do so because they want something from me. It isn't a symbiotic exchange; rather, they want to feed off me or fill up their cup. No thanks: My cup is fine bone china, babe, and I'm careful who interacts with it.

Mentors

The Universe, or whatever you want to call it, has a weird way of working life out and helping you. You can call it destiny, fate, coincidence, paths crossing—you know all the sayings. Sometimes, there are early childhood mentors or people who come into your life to show you what life can be like.

I was meant to live in Rosedale Drive in the few years that led up to my parents' divorce. It was a beautiful street. Trees lined each side of the road. It was just green and leafy. It was my favorite home out of all our homes. We moved a lot; my siblings and mom would say it was because my dad couldn't pay the mortgage, and yes, that was definitely a part of it, but actually... my mom was a gypsy. She was so unhappy inside and she loved a change; she loved to move house. She would often walk through "show houses" to get ideas. My mom, like all of us, had a dream in her head, a dream that was alive inside of her.

Rosedale Drive led us to our neighbors Liz and Andre Yates.

Liz's home was this peaceful kaleidoscope of color and love, all mushed into one. Even the air smelt different at Liz's house. Her beautiful daughter was my cheeky friend Anna. I used to race up to Anna's house to play in the afternoons after school.

I was able to be a carefree child at Liz's house. Her beautiful blonde hair and her calm demeanor would float through the air as she cooked in the kitchen or passed through the house checking on us playing.

She was uncomplicated, smart, fancy, and so kind. I saw how she was a mother, and it embedded in me how I wanted to be as a mom one day to my own "Anna."

I could see that reflected in Anna. Anna was just gorgeous. Still is.

Liz became good friends with my mom. It was fate. They would walk to church together, and soon a tight friendship had formed.

But soon, just like all the others, that friendship came to a crossroads when Liz showed me support and offered for me to stay in her home while I commuted out of town to complete my law conversions.

Liz and Mom broke up. No surprises why.

But as fate would have it, as I got older, despite our age difference, Liz and I became besties. We didn't connect because of the soreness caused by Sylvia's venom or because we had both lost someone we loved, but because we actually had so much soul connection. We are on each other's vibe and we operate at the same energy frequency. If our friendship was a radio station, I would be listening all day. Liz is on my "super top people" list. It's a divine connection.

She's part of my chosen pack. And it is a full circle of destiny, in that indirectly my mom introduced me to Liz, and me playing in Liz's pool as a child with my gorgeous friend Anna, all those years ago, was a precursor to the adult bond that would be formed later.

Other Extended Family Members

Another Universe intervention was my aunt Debra. Debra was my mother's half-sister and so had been raised differently from my mom. Debra taught me how to be a girl. She introduced me to the worldlier, finer things in life. I observed her impeccable taste in fashion, art, decor, and travel and her career in law. I liked what I saw and I took great inspiration from her. She loved me unconditionally and always let me into her home, even when she was battling her own demons with a husband who didn't appreciate her or a baby daughter who had severe reflux. Debra always believed me about mom, and she recognized that my siblings were my mom's pack of followers. How comforting it was to feel that I had an adult understand me back then, and to provide hope and inspiration for what my future life could be.

Having childhood role models or mentors, these wonderful destiny-ordained encounters, are what can get a young girl through.

Do you have any that you can recognize in your own life? Those may be some of your people, and it's important, if you are an aunt or if you come into contact with young women, to always treat them with respect and to believe them when they share their stories with you. You may be their mentor one day.

Chapter 10:

Decision Time—Should I Stay or Should I Go?

Let everything happen to you.
Beauty and terror.
Just keep going.
No feeling is final.

–Rainer Maria Rilke

There's a special kind of hell that comes with having a narcissistic mother. It's a world where every day feels like a battle, where you're constantly walking on eggshells, trying to avoid setting off a landmine. It's exhausting, it's infuriating, and it can leave you feeling like you're losing your damn mind.

But here's the thing: You're not alone. There are so many of us, male and female. There are so many other daughters out there who know exactly what you're going through. They've lived through the same mind games, the same manipulation, the same constant criticism and belittling. And they've come out the other side, standing strong.

It's important to recognize that when it comes to dealing with a toxic or narcissistic mother, there are generally two options: Either you can try and manage the relationship, or you can break up with your mother:

- **Managing the relationship:** This involves setting clear boundaries, limiting contact, and emotionally distancing yourself while still maintaining some level of connection. This option may be feasible if your mother is willing to respect your boundaries and if the relationship isn't causing you significant harm.

- **Breaking up and leaving:** This means completely cutting off contact with your mother, as I did. This option is often necessary when the relationship is consistently abusive, toxic, and detrimental to your well-being, and when your mother is unwilling to change or respect your boundaries.

Managing the Relationship

First and foremost, you need to accept reality. Your mother is who she is, and she's unlikely to change. No matter how much you wish things were different, no matter how much you hope that one day she'll wake up and realize the error of her ways, it's probably not going to happen. Narcissists are notoriously resistant to change, and they often lack the self-awareness and empathy needed to truly understand the impact of their behavior on others.

So, what can you do? Set boundaries. Establish clear limits on what you will and will not tolerate from your mother. This might mean limiting contact, refusing to engage in certain topics of conversation, or even cutting ties altogether if necessary. It's not easy, but it's essential for your own well-being.

Your mother needs to know what is acceptable and what is not, and you need to be very clear on it. Unwavering. Do not be inconsistent and allow something to happen one week and then change it up the next. Narcissistic mothers are like "upset children." They will push the boundaries to get what they want. You need to take control in these situations and have a strong internal compass about what is okay and what is not okay.

Treat your mother as you would a tantruming toddler or a disrespectful work colleague. Practice common phrases that can be used on high-conflict people so that you're prepared and ready when she oversteps the mark. Narcissists know you well and will recognize when you are vulnerable, and they will try and strike your old wounds. So, you have to be trained and mentally fit for this.

Communicating your boundaries to your narcissistic mother can be one of the most daunting parts of this process. You know she won't take it well. You can anticipate the rage, the guilt-tripping, the gaslighting. This is where scripts can be incredibly helpful. Plan out exactly what you want to say and practice it beforehand. Write it down and edit it until it feels clear and concise.

When crafting your script, stick to "I" statements. This keeps the focus on your feelings and decisions, rather than accusing or blaming. For example:

"Mom, I've decided that for my own well-being, I need to set some boundaries in our relationship. Moving forward, I will not tolerate any comments about my weight or appearance. If it happens, I will end the conversation immediately. I'm also not available for calls after 8 p.m. I need you to respect these boundaries. If you can't, I'll have to take a step back from our relationship. This isn't up for discussion. I hope you can understand."

Notice how this script is clear, direct, and non-negotiable. You're not asking for her approval or leaving room for debate. You're stating your needs and the consequences if they're not met.

When you deliver your script, try to do so in a calm, neutral tone. This can be incredibly challenging in the face of your mother's reactions, but it's important to maintain control of the conversation. If she starts to yell, gaslight, or guilt-trip you, calmly repeat your boundaries and end the conversation if necessary: "Mom, I've stated my boundaries. I'm not going to argue about this. I need to go now."

Even with the clearest communication, your narcissistic mother is unlikely to respect your boundaries without a fight. Prepare yourself for the typical arsenal of manipulation tactics (Jabeen et al., 2021):

- **Rage and aggression:** She may scream, yell, call you names, or even get physically intimidating. This is a tactic designed to scare you into compliance.

- **Sulking and silent treatment:** When you set boundaries or refuse to engage in her manipulative tactics, your mother may resort to sulking or giving you the silent treatment. She may withdraw affection or communication as a way to punish you and make you feel guilty for not complying with her wishes.

- **Guilt-tripping:** Your mother may try to guilt-trip you into complying with her demands by emphasizing how much she's sacrificed for you in the past or how ungrateful you are for not meeting her expectations. She may play on your sense of obligation, using phrases like "After all I've done for you..." or "You're breaking your mother's heart..." She may lay on the guilt thickly, telling you how much you're hurting her and how, after everything she's done for you, this is how you repay her.

- **Playing the victim:** She may twist the situation to make herself the victim and you the aggressor. She may cry and lament about what a terrible daughter you are, and how no one understands her pain.

- **Gaslighting:** She may also use gaslighting to make you question your own perceptions, memories, and sanity. She may deny events that occurred, twist your words, or accuse you of being too sensitive or overreacting when you express your feelings or concerns. She may tell you that it wasn't that bad or that you're remembering things wrong.

- **Triangulation:** Your narcissistic mother may attempt to triangulate you with other family members, pitting you against each other or creating alliances to isolate and control you. She may share private information or twist your words to create conflict and maintain her position of power.

- **Flying monkeys:** Alternatively, she may enlist other family members or friends to pressure you on her behalf. They may give you messages about how much your mother is suffering, how unforgiving you're being.

- **Smear campaigns:** If you continue to resist her control or set firm boundaries, your mother may engage in smear campaigns, spreading lies or exaggerations about you to other family members, friends, or even on social media. This is an attempt to discredit you and paint herself as the victim.

Knowing these tactics can help you spot them when they happen. Remind yourself that this is a predictable pattern of behavior for a narcissist who's losing control. It's not a reflection of you being a bad daughter or your boundaries being unreasonable. You are simply refusing to be mistreated any longer.

Have some phrases to have ready to shut down these tactics:

- "I'm not going to argue about this."
- "My decision is not up for discussion."
- "I'm sorry you feel that way, but I need to do what's best for me."
- "I'm not responsible for your feelings."
- "If you continue to yell, I'm going to hang up/leave."

Remember, you don't have to justify, argue, defend, or explain (JADE). Your boundaries are not a negotiation.

Another key strategy is to avoid seeking validation from your mother. Narcissistic mothers are often incapable of providing the kind of unconditional love and support that children need. They may withhold affection or approval as a means of control, leaving you constantly feeling like you're not good enough. But here's the thing: You are good enough, and your worth is not dependent on your mother's opinion of you; anyway, you know by now that she has bad opinions! Focus on building your own self-esteem and surrounding yourself with people who truly appreciate and support you.

When conflicts do arise (and they will), try to avoid engaging in arguments with your mother. Narcissists thrive on drama and conflict, and she may use arguments as a way to manipulate or control you. Instead, try to remain calm and use phrases like "I understand your perspective" or "Let's agree to disagree" to de-escalate the situation. It's not about letting her win; it's about protecting your own emotional well-being.

Self-care is also crucial when dealing with your narcissistic mother. Make time for activities that bring you joy and help you relax. Seek out supportive relationships with friends, partners, or therapists who can provide a listening ear and help you process your experiences. Remember, you deserve to be happy and healthy, regardless of your relationship with your mother.

Finally, don't be afraid to seek professional help if you need it. Dealing with a narcissistic parent can be incredibly challenging, and it's okay to admit that you need support. A therapist who specializes in narcissistic family dynamics can provide valuable insights and tools for navigating this complex relationship.

It's important to be aware of the different psychological reactions, listed above, that narcissistic mothers may exhibit when you don't comply with their demands or expectations. These reactions can include further attempts at control, manipulation, isolation, and other toxic behaviors.

At the end of the day, managing a relationship with a narcissistic mother is a lifelong journey. There will be ups and downs, victories and setbacks. But by prioritizing your own well-being, setting healthy boundaries, and surrounding yourself with supportive people, you can achieve a manageable relationship that is fair to you and that you find acceptable and comfortable.

Breaking Up

I am not a huge fan of social media—surprisingly, as during my tumultuous years I used to be very active on platforms such as Facebook and Instagram, frantically posting all sorts of things. I now cringe at how I used to do that and my need to share banal details about my holidays, changes in jobs, or pictures of seasonal flooding rains in my backyard! Who cares?

Now, in my quieter years, I don't have Facebook, and I only use Instagram to get décor and gardening ideas, as well as find some good poets. But I do remember a meme I saw years ago that I loved, as it resonated so strongly with me. It went something like this: "Don't wait till your death bed to tell people how you feel. Tell them to fuck off now."

I liked that.

Women break up with friends, boyfriends, hairdressers, and therapists. Some wives divorce their husbands after a few months or 30 years. Deciding to leave a relationship or a connection is something that is encouraged in society nowadays, and many advocate for it as a win for your mental health. Don't stay in something that is causing you pain and stopping you from growing as a person. So, why do some of us feel like it's taboo to break up with a parent? To end the relationship for good, to not be friends with your ex-mom, but to close the relationship and have no contact at all?

There are several reasons why breaking up with a parent can feel more difficult and more taboo than ending other types of relationships (Agllias, 2016):

- **Societal expectations:** Society places a high value on the parent–child relationship, often viewing it as sacred and unbreakable. There is an expectation that children should honor and respect their parents no matter what, making it emotionally challenging to go against this norm.

- **Guilt and obligation:** Many people feel a strong sense of guilt or obligation toward their parents, even if the relationship is toxic or abusive. There may be a fear of being seen as ungrateful or disloyal for cutting ties.

- **Hope for change:** Unlike other relationships, where it may be easier to accept that the other person is unlikely to change, children often hold onto the hope that their parent will eventually become the loving, supportive figure they desire. This hope can make it harder to let go.

- **Family pressure:** Breaking up with a parent can lead to pressure and judgment from other family members, who may not understand or support the decision. The fear of losing relationships with siblings, grandparents, or other relatives can make it feel like an impossibly high cost.

- **Lack of understanding:** Because breaking up with a parent is less common and less openly discussed than other types of breakups, people who make this choice may feel isolated and misunderstood. Others may question their decision or assume they are overreacting without fully grasping the depth of pain and dysfunction in the relationship.

My mother was my biggest heartbreak. Past romantic breakups had nothing on the pain I felt on breaking up with her the first time—because, you know, in an abusive relationship you can go back many times, as you hope like hell that the person will change. I know this professionally—I am a domestic violence lawyer and see women as well as other family members return to their abuser for many different reasons. No judgment.

While I could see that these women should never return to their relationships, I knew that within days, weeks, or months they might return, trying to save the marriage or relationship, and my clients would be faced with the same painful situation again.

There was a beautiful young girl named Susan who came into my office with her blonde, cherubic-looking baby. Susan was seeking a permanent protection order and for her to be granted a relocation order so she could move back to New Zealand with her baby. It is a rare thing for the courts to grant relocation orders; it is very difficult to persuade them to allow this, especially when the baby is so young and probably wouldn't be able to forge a relationship with the father, which the courts like to encourage between children and each parent. Susan had been regularly beaten, raped, strangled, and emotionally gaslit by her husband, and she sat in my office holding her angelic child, retelling her story to me.

Through various support networks, our firm managed the unthinkable. We persuaded the courts to let her return to her country of birth with no restrictions on her to return the baby or allow contact with the father. It was a rare victory in relocation matters in family law. But this masterful manipulative fuckwit managed to persuade Susan that they were a young family and he would change. He begged her not to leave the country. He looked as angelic as the baby, and was well-dressed, with curly blond hair, a slim build, and big doe eyes. I used to stare at him from a distance in court and think that he looked like the good guy next door or a Hugo Boss model. Unfortunately, Susan withdrew the domestic violence protection order and went quiet on me.

On a random Wednesday afternoon, I was walking up to the courts, which were on a busy main road near a small shopping mall, to lodge some more domestic violence applications, and I saw her with him and the baby. She saw me, and I read the fear in her eyes. She looked nervous and immediately put her head down and turned away, and we passed each other like two ships in the night. I often think of Susan and her gorgeous baby and ponder her "sliding doors" moment, when she was at the crossroads of a life-altering decision that could have changed her and her young baby's life for the better.

Domestic violence is a complicated dynamic, and I understand why women leave and also why they return to their abusive partners. I hold no judgment. But, just like we tell these women who are being gaslit and exploited that they don't deserve that treatment and that the crap they are being told about themselves by their emotionally abusive partners is not true, we understand without reservation why they can't leave, and we don't question why they want to leave.

Even with my teenagers, I tell them that if a friendship is becoming destructive and they are starting to get the feeling that it has run its course and it's time to end it, they should trust their gut and end the destructive energy exchange. Because relationships are all about energy exchanges.

Despite the challenges, it's important to remember that you have the right to protect your emotional well-being and set boundaries in any relationship, including with a parent. It's not about assigning blame or seeking to punish, but rather about prioritizing your own healing and growth.

Breaking Free: Going No Contact With a Narcissistic Mother

So, how do you break free? How do you weather the storm of your mother's manipulation and stand firm in your decision to protect yourself? It takes courage, determination, and a deep commitment to your own well-being. It's not an easy path, but it's a necessary one for your healing and growth.

First, get clear on your reasons. Before you make the decision to go no contact, it's crucial to get crystal clear about why you are doing so. This isn't about a single argument or a momentary frustration; it's about a pattern of behavior that has consistently undermined your well-being. Take the time to reflect on the impact your mother's narcissistic behavior has had on your life, your relationships, and your sense of self.

Remember, breaking up with a toxic parent is not about being a "bad" son or daughter; it's about choosing to break free from a cycle of abuse and dysfunction. It's a courageous act of self-love and a powerful step toward reclaiming your life. You are not responsible for your mother's happiness or well-being. That's her job, not yours.

Next, block and delete if necessary. If your mother refuses to respect your boundaries despite clear communication, you may need to take more drastic measures to protect yourself. This can include:

- blocking her number and email
- blocking her on social media
- asking your partner or a friend to screen your calls
- moving without giving her your new address
- considering a restraining order if her behavior becomes threatening

These measures can feel extreme and even cruel. You may worry about how she'll cope without you or what others will think. But remember, you're not doing this to punish her. You're doing this to protect yourself from further abuse. You have the right to set boundaries and prioritize your own well-being, even if others don't understand or approve.

You have the right to feel safe and at peace in your own life. If your mother's behavior is constantly disrupting that safety and peace, you have every right to limit or end contact with her. This is the natural consequence of her actions, not you being cruel. It's not about blame or revenge, but about taking the necessary steps to protect yourself and create a healthier, happier life.

You will also need to surround yourself with support. Going no contact with a narcissistic mother can be incredibly isolating. Other family members may not understand or support your decision. They may pressure you to reconcile or accuse you of tearing the family apart. This is where having a strong support network is essential. Don't try to navigate this journey alone.

Seek out people who validate your experiences and respect your choices. This might include:

- a therapist specializing in narcissistic abuse recovery
- support groups for adult children of narcissists (online or in person)
- friends who have gone through similar experiences
- your partner or spouse

Lean on these people when the guilt and self-doubt creep in. Let them remind you of your strength, your worth, and the validity of your choices. Allow yourself to be vulnerable and share your struggles. You don't have to put on a brave face all the time. It's okay to admit that this is hard and to ask for help when you need it.

Creating this circle of support can also help counteract the negative messages you've internalized from your mother. Surrounding yourself with people who truly love and appreciate you can be a powerful antidote to the years of criticism and put-downs. It can help you rebuild your sense of self-worth and learn to trust your own perceptions and feelings again.

As you navigate the process of breaking free from your narcissistic mother, focusing on self-care should be your top priority. You've spent so long focused on her needs, her feelings, her reactions. Now it's time to turn that energy inward. This is your opportunity to nurture yourself and discover who you are outside of your mother's influence.

Self-care looks different for everyone. It might include:

- going to therapy to process your emotions and learn new coping strategies

- journaling to gain clarity and insight into your experiences
- engaging in hobbies and activities that bring you joy and fulfillment
- spending time in nature to ground yourself and find peace
- practicing mindfulness and meditation to manage stress and anxiety
- nurturing your body with healthy food, exercise, and rest

Beyond self-care, this is also a time for self-discovery and rebuilding. When you've grown up with a narcissistic mother, your sense of self can be deeply fractured. You may have trouble knowing who you are, what you want, and even what you like and dislike outside of her influence. This is your chance to get to know yourself on a deeper level and build a life that truly reflects your authentic self.

Use this time to get curious about yourself. Explore your passions, try new things, and question your beliefs. Surround yourself with people and experiences that make you feel alive and true to yourself. This is a journey of reclaiming your identity, your autonomy, and your right to a life free from abuse and manipulation.

This is your chance to rewrite your story. You get to decide what kind of life you want to create, what kind of person you want to be. It's a journey of reclaiming your autonomy, your voice, and your very selfhood. It won't be easy, and there will be setbacks along the way. But every step you take toward healing and self-discovery is a step toward a brighter, healthier future.

Remember, breaking free from a narcissistic mother is not a one-time event. It's a process of learning, unlearning, healing, and growing. There will be setbacks and challenges along the way. You may doubt yourself, fall back into old patterns, or feel tempted to break your no contact rule. This is all part of the journey. Be patient with yourself, and remember that healing is not a linear process.

As the poet Nayyirah Waheed writes, "i am mine before i am anyone else's" (Waheed, n.d.). You belong to yourself first and foremost. You have the right to protect your peace and to surround yourself with people who truly love and support you. This is your life, your journey, and you get to decide what it looks like.

Going no contact is not about punishment or revenge. It's about giving yourself the space to heal and to break free from the cycle of abuse. It's a reclamation of your autonomy and your right to be treated with respect and kindness. It's a powerful act of self-love and a declaration that you will no longer tolerate being mistreated, even by your own mother.

People are shocked when I say I broke up with my mother. But people are never shocked if you tell them you got a divorce or left a bitchy friendship. But your mother? Ouch. *Who's the bitch? You or her?* they probably think.

I used to carry such pain in my heart when I first broke up with my mother. It was like losing the love of my life. I did really truly love her, and I wanted her to love me.

These milestones would happen for me, like when I went back to university in my early 30s and did my international conversions in Australia. As I drove back from writing my last exam, the sun was setting orange and I was sitting in traffic. The song "Hello" by Adele came on the radio. It talks about reaching out to someone from your past but never quite reconnecting due to either moving on or realizing that the relationship has changed and doesn't fit into your current life. The line that always got me was when Adele sang, "I'm sorry for breaking your heart, but it don't matter, it clearly doesn't tear you apart any more." Every time my mother would try to reconnect with me (to satisfy her own needs), I realized I had become indifferent toward her.

It was an aching pain. I missed my mother as if she had died. I mourned her. When I used to listen to that song, it felt half like me speaking to her and half like her speaking to me. In the end, if my mother ever reached out, it wouldn't tear me apart anymore. It's important, if you do break up with your mom, that you mourn the loss of her. Celebrate the good times and perhaps mourn the loss of the mother that you wish she could have been.

At first, when I broke up with my mother, she would not take no for an answer. So, I had to digitally block her on email, social media, and my phone. She then tried to send me a soppy, manipulative birthday card in the post with some pics of me as a child sitting on her lap. She had sent them to my husband's business address as that was all she had. I looked at them and put them in the bin. I was calm but peaceful. I saw through the manipulation.

Before I threw them away, I stared at the images of me as a beautiful young girl. I didn't like the way my eyes as a child looked in those pictures, because I could recognize the unease as I sat on her lap and I knew how I would have been feeling inside. She now does not know my physical address.

She tells my siblings that she is "hurting." She runs me down to my gentle sister, who is too weak and scared to stand up to her, but never utters any criticism of me to my brothers (that I'm aware of) as she knows she won't get a reaction from them. She still picks her audience to this day. My mother does not respect boundaries and will only try and contact me to make herself feel better about being a mother, not because she is seeking me out to love me.

She does not like telling people that only three out of her four children speak to her. That reflects badly on her, so she tells everyone that I have bad mental health. That's her scapegoat. Supposedly, according to Sylvia's brain, I'm bipolar—although, and I write this with the highest degree of sarcasm, I don't ever recall being diagnosed! I do laugh about that "diagnosis" now, as it is so far from the truth. The only bipolar woman in this family is perhaps her. The hypocrisy used to burn me, but now it's like reading the tabloids: You know it's bullshit and you turn the page.

There was always something, but it was never her. I stopped feeling the need to defend or justify myself. I adopted the motto of the late Queen Elizabeth II: "Never complain, never explain." I knew who I was. I could feel it. I was intelligent, emotionally intuitive, and sick of her going down her rabbit hole and dragging me with her.

She went from being the toxic love of my life to the wreck of my life. She was like the boyfriend you want to spend all your time with and adore, but then you realize he's a dud and you can't break up with him quickly enough. I was so done with this mess. I saw an interview where a young girl asked an elder, "How much disrespect do I take before I cut off a family member or friend?" and he responded, "How much poison do you take before you die?"

In my childhood, my adulthood, and even my early motherhood, my mother intimidated me because I didn't want to upset her. I was so nervous of her. But then I realized that she wasn't this powerful monster; she was just a weak coward who needed to go. Like a child who believes monsters are living in their cupboards or under their beds: When kids face their monsters and open the cupboard or check underneath the bed, they are hit with reality. It's not a monster, it's a pair of shoes!

The straw that broke the camel's back was me in a "Sylvia attempt stage," when I was trying to manage the relationship. I was making idle chit-chat with her over text messages (I couldn't really talk to her freely about much as she was unpredictable, so we kept to shallow, safe topics). To provide context, we were discussing our homes. Because my mother lives in another country to me and I hadn't seen her new home, I asked her to show me a picture of her favorite place in her house—one that made her happy. My mom loved to decorate, so this was a good question, I thought. *Silly me.*

I thought maybe she would show me her garden, or a kitchen windowsill with her favorite teacup, or some god-awful antique spoons from her husband's dead mother... but no.

Sylvia dished me a winner.

There I was, sitting in my car outside my children's school, thinking my mother was going to send back a photo of her favorite doily or her red wine collection. And my mind drifted off while waiting for the pic. I was thinking about my grocery list and needing to buy lactose-free milk and cat biscuits on the way home. Arbitrary stuff. The high-pitched ding signaling a message on WhatsApp broke my thoughts.

Sylvia sent back a photo of the mantelpiece in her lounge. That was her favorite place in her new home. At first glance, I thought, *How nice, mom.*

However, on closer inspection, as I pinched the photograph to zoom in, I saw on the mantelpiece numerous photographs of all my siblings, their partners, and their children. Multiple. It was a big mantelpiece, so there was enough space.

There were none of me, my husband, or my children. Nothing. It was like I didn't exist. My life didn't make it onto her mantelpiece.

I sat there and, suddenly, my need to buy lactose-free milk and cat biscuits on the way home was shattered. The school bell rang, breaking the silence.

I sat in my car, thinking, *How—fucking—rude of you.*

How dare you.

Unless she had had lost all her eyesight and brain function, any reasonable mother would work out pretty quickly that her fourth child and grandchildren were not on the prized mantelpiece with everyone else. *Everyone else.*

Her favorite place in her home was that. This was not an oversight; it was a direct stab wound through my jugular in retaliation for the on–off relationship that I was trying to manage. She was punishing me. When I asked her where we were on the mantelpiece, she gaslit me and told me I was overreacting and that our family was elsewhere.

I sat there and thought, *This isn't good enough for me.*

I deserve better.

I realized that I had outgrown her. This was pathetic and childish. And as Taylor Swift would say, *"We are never ever ever getting back together."*

If that was my daughter and someone was dishonoring her like that, playing nasty mind games, teasing her, and taunting her, I would tell her to get away from that person. Permanently. Never to be repeated again.

I model behavior to my children that I think will keep them grounded and resilient through life's challenges. Ending relationships and friendships and leaving unhealthy jobs is a lesson and a skill to be practiced.

What am I teaching my children if I stay and tolerate abuse? What message am I sending them? That it's okay to have someone pick on you, belittle you, torment you, and criticize you?

And that because they are family, your blood relation, you must invite them for Christmas, invite them into your home to eat your roast turkey and hold hands at the table saying grace?

No.

It stops with me.

Relationships are an exchange. I treat you well, you treat me well. If not, then off you go, buddy. I model self-love and self-respect to my children. Not martyrdom.

This is where I left my mother.

Chapter 11:

This Stops With Me

There's a saying that loosely says that the storms you face should not get your kids wet. I'm not sure who said it first, but that message strongly resonated with me early on in my life and lived in me when I was pregnant with my son and daughter. I made a conscious decision to be their gatekeeper—to keep my past from them, and to not imbue my mother's dysfunction by mimicking it and letting it seep into my beautiful children's lives.

I have a son whom I adore; he was born to be my first lesson in love and motherhood and my first experience of life testing me to see if I would repeat the generational trauma. My son, when born, was a glorious gift who came to me as a 7 lb 11 oz love vessel on a rainy Wednesday morning. He marked the start of a new age.

I have relished being "his mom," his first female friend, and making memories with him. He is the male version of me, and I love his foresight and emotional intelligence; he always shares his fast food takeaways with me, lets me nibble on some of his chips, and offers to make me cups of tea when he gets home from school in the afternoon. Aside from his dad, he is the first to wrap his arms around me when I'm upset.

He is 18 years old now. Although the years have flown by, as they do, I understand that our children are not our possessions and our time is long but short; I have accepted that he can go and venture out into the world whenever he is ready and step into his destiny. I wouldn't dream of holding him back with my past trauma. He is my oath keeper and the wisest version of my younger self. He is the wood element of my earth.

And so, the life cycle continues... but he is not going off limping into the world with Mother Wounds.

Because it stopped with me.

Breaking the Cycle: More Than Just Avoiding Abuse

Breaking generational cycles goes far deeper than just avoiding the obvious forms of abuse. It means examining every inherited pattern, every unquestioned tradition, every "that's just how we do things" moment. As cycle breakers, we must question everything we learned about parenting, asking ourselves: "Is this truly beneficial for my child, or am I just repeating what was done to me?"

Sometimes, these patterns are subtle. It might be pushing our children into activities we never got to do, living vicariously through their achievements in sports or academics. Maybe we weren't allowed to quit the swim team, so now we force our children to persist in activities they hate. Or perhaps we inherited rigid beliefs about food—"Clean your plate, there are starving children"—born from our parents' experiences of scarcity, but creating unhealthy relationships with food in the next generation.

Religious traditions, too, often need examining. Many adult children of narcissists find themselves questioning the strict religious practices they were raised with, choosing to raise their own children with more spiritual freedom. This decision often faces fierce resistance from family members who see it as rejecting their values rather than protecting the next generation from religious trauma.

To break these cycles effectively, we must reflect deeply on our own childhood experiences. Ask yourself:

- What parenting practices made you feel ashamed, fearful, or unloved?

- When did you feel your confidence being crushed?

- What would you have needed to feel secure and supported?

- Which family traditions actually served you, and which ones caused harm?

Some might argue that we should excuse toxic parenting if our parents were themselves abuse survivors. "They did the best they could with what they knew," they say. But understanding the origin of abuse doesn't justify its continuation. Yes, our parents may have been damaged by their own experiences, but they still had choices. We all do. That's precisely why breaking the cycle is so crucial—because we can choose differently.

When I look at my children, I see the opportunity to create new patterns, healthier traditions. Each interaction is a chance to ask myself, "Am I parenting from a place of conscious choice, or am I just repeating what was done to me?"

This chapter, though, is specifically about my daughter, because daughters can trigger their toxic mothers just by virtue of being female. I was blessed to have a daughter who helped me be the mom to her that I always wanted for myself. Reader, you may have children yourself and be able to relate to this strong maternal instinct, or maybe you don't have children for whatever reason, but the mission is clear: Do not pollute the future generation of children, step-children, or any young people.

I recall standing in my kitchen, pregnant with my daughter, talking to my mother. "I need to look into her eyes; I need to meet her," I said, thinking about my desire to have a little girl. I felt so ashamed being pregnant, grossly overweight, and hated the sight of myself. But I envisioned this little girl I would have, her eyes staring into mine, trusting me, knowing that I would be her mentor for life. I got tearful in front of my mother.

She laughed. "Oh, you're being silly. Stop being so emotional," she said, dismissing my feelings and minimizing my yearning for unconditional love. But I had a bigger, more wholesome vision. A few months previously, I had suffered a miscarriage while flying back from a trip to Australia. Sylvia had dismissed my significant loss as merely losing a "fetus," not a "real baby." I knew inside that this pregnancy was going to be healthy and that my little girl would come.

Reader, I did meet my daughter. I stared into her eyes as she lay in the hospital crib and I returned her wide-eyed gaze with a promise that I would never be the villain in her life. That I would celebrate her, dote on her, protect her, and love her—unconditionally.

We were right at the beginning of our relationship, *just she and I.*

Me loving my daughter unconditionally was also a chance to love myself unconditionally. I was going to heal that fractured and scared inner child who didn't get to have a loving mom.

This is where the past was left in the past, where it stopped with me and did not trespass onto my magnificent girl.

My daughter is now 15 years old. She is everything I wish I could've been: brilliant, witty, intelligent, mischievous, kind, and strong-willed. No one messes with her. She's got her feet planted firmly on the ground, and when she feels unsteady, I'm right beside her, ready to be her sounding board and to celebrate her. I call her my "steel marshmallow," a term King Charles III uses to describe The Princess of Wales. My girlie is feminine and kind on the outside, dodging stepping on garden snails in the rain, but inside, she stands firm in her beliefs and weathers life's storms with calm measure and graceful composure. I admire her.

Her hair is shiny and silky, and I take her to the hair salon to discuss new styles, or we try a few things at home. I laughed when she tried to cut her fringe herself and then came to me seeking advice on how to correct it! I love the way she ices her face in the morning using my baking bowl to reduce her puffy eyes and details the drama of the day for 55 minutes as we drive home from school. She has taught me about eyelash lifts, TikTok, and ridiculous teenage acronyms, which every now and again I use by default with my academic colleagues at the university where I work!

I pay attention to her adolescent skin upsets, and listen to her and believe her when she tells me how heavy and painful her monthly periods are. I leave her love notes under her pillow and in her lunch box. I danced and sang with her at the Taylor Swift Era's concert until our voices were no more, and we fell asleep on each other's shoulders on the train home.

I cherish the moments when she wants to go for long drives, just to talk. I celebrate her stunning beauty, her gorgeous legs, and her close bond with her father and brother.

I sacrifice my time with her so her dad can drive her to school every morning, because she needs her dad, and he adores her.

I love her unrestrained dreams and how she wants to study overseas but still wants to take her cat with her!

I love walking hand in hand with her, or glancing across a room and seeing her engaging with people. The way her perfume fills up our home and the way she doesn't return my shampoo, conditioner, or Dior lip gloss.

I take her to extra French and Mandarin lessons, because she loves to learn languages, and I patiently wait for her to go through any out-there fashion phases or friendships that don't honor her.

I respect her body and knock on her bedroom door.

I let her be, in her world, and I meet her there.

I love her without reservation.

Without condition.

No terms or hidden clauses attached or typed in fine print.

Most importantly, I say sorry to her when I stuff up or act impulsively without hearing her out before judging a situation.

I say sorry, and I mean it.

Because I am not perfect, but I'll hold myself accountable, and I will always go and knock on her bedroom door and ask if she will hear me out when she's upset with me. She is like cool mint ice tea, delicious in every way, and I am in awe of her.

I am not a version of my ex-mother.

I am me; I am my children's loving and devoted "Mumzee."

Chapter 12:

This Is Where I Leave You

There is a practice in Ireland that speaks of ushering in the new and pushing out the old. That on New Year's Eve, you should leave your front door open to let the new year in and open your back door to let the old year and all its memories, good and bad, leave and be put to rest.

I like that, because I like moving on. I'm not going to sit in sorrow or anger; I believe in taking up the challenge of life and adapting and rising higher than before. I love looking back at life's changing narratives and how the black sheep, with hard work, eventually becomes the shepherd.

You know by now that I love music, and I turned to it a lot for solace and to gain perspective—and still do. The song "The Great War" by Taylor Swift speaks about two sparring lovers and how emotionally taxing it was. She relates it to a war and uses different war analogies. Words like: "My knuckles were bruised like violets," "Maybe it was ego swinging, maybe it was her, Flashes of the battle come back to me in a blur," and "Broken and blue, so I called off the troops."

I used to have such rage for my mom. I used to fight with her in my sleep and wake up feeling agitated, and would carry that through my day. I used to imagine slapping her.

No, I'll be honest: punching her.

The rage came from deep-seeded pain, slow-turning hurt.

Now, in my quiet era, the rage has gone. Quite literally, the demon that occupied my mind has drifted away. It knows it has no space to gas out my mind. My body feels lighter, my lungs have more space, and I feel like I have room to breathe.

I hear, via the family grapevine, that my mother plans to visit Australia when her third husband passes away. No doubt she will pack her red wine and come across to fulfill her duty as the doting mother of three out of four, who takes a 27-hour flight to see her darlings.

Not me. My mom is on my "never to repeat" people list. My mom lives in the UK, and I live in Australia. It is her loss, not being in my life and not knowing me, not mine.

The true power of boundaries lies not in the walls they create, but in the peace they bring. When you finally understand who you are and what you want from life, setting boundaries becomes as natural as breathing. It's no longer about anger or retaliation—it's simply about protecting your peace.

I've learned that indifference is the healthiest place to land after trauma. The rage that once consumed me, that had me waking up with clenched fists and grinding teeth, has transformed into something quieter, more powerful. It's not that I've forgotten; it's that I've transcended. I've reached a state of peaceful detachment where my mother's actions no longer have the power to disturb my inner calm.

This peace comes from being grounded in who I am and where I'm heading. When you're secure in your own truth, when you know your worth and your direction, nothing can shake you—not even the person who once had the power to shatter your world. Every decision I make now comes from a place of self-respect and self-love, choosing what brings peace rather than chaos into my life.

Some might mistake this for coldness, but it's quite the opposite. It's about being so deeply rooted in your own well-being that you no longer need to engage with what hurts you. There's a profound difference between carrying anger and maintaining boundaries. Anger keeps you tethered to the past, while boundaries free you to move forward.

She has lost out on loving me and having a daughter, a best friend, to love her and steady her as she gets older and as she nears the end. I do not feel anything toward her. The emotions do not stir in my body or pound in my chest.

My husband has asked what I will do when the time comes and I get the call that Sylvia has passed away, or that she is sick and on her death bed.

"Do you want to say goodbye?" I have pondered how I would feel.

If she suddenly passes away and I get the call, I will say to whichever sibling has notified me, "I'm sorry for *your* loss." I've already mourned. And I mourned hard.

I lost my mom a long time ago. She died a long time ago, in my mind and heart. And I am at peace with that.

If, on the other hand, she was dying in a hospital bed and asked for me, would I go and see her?

I ask myself, would I only stand at the door and watch her sleep?

Or...

Would I go up to her, stroke her hair, and tell her that I hope she finally finds the peace she needed to find so many years ago?

I would wish her well into the next realm, wherever, whatever that may be.

I would thank her for being my greatest, worst teacher. Because only through this experience of having her as my fractured mother did I really hone my skills of resilience.

I was resilient from the start of my life. And only with her always pushing against me and stunting me did I really sharpen my weapon, which was resilience.

I would quietly say to her, "You're safe; it's over now."

And leave.

References

Adele. (2015). Hello [Song]. On *25*. XL Recordings.

Agllias, K. (2016). Disconnection and decision-making: Adult children explain their reasons for estranging from parents. *Australian Social Work, 69*(1), 92–104. https://doi.org/10.1080/0312407X.2015.1004355

Alcott, L. (n.d.). *In a toxic family system, the black sheep is often.* The Minds Journal. https://themindsjournal.com/quotes/in-a-toxic-family-system-the-black-sheep-is-often/

American Psychiatric Association. (2013). *Diagnostic and statistical manual of mental disorders* (5th ed.). Pearson.

Baker, A. J. L., & Ben-Ami, N. (2011). To turn a child against a parent is to turn a child against himself: The direct and indirect effects of exposure to parental alienation strategies on self-esteem and well-being. *Journal of Divorce & Remarriage, 52*(7), 472–489. https://doi.org/10.1080/10502556.2011.609424

Bancroft, L. (n.d.). *Lundy Bancroft quote.* Goodreads. https://www.goodreads.com/quotes/8705599-abuse-grows-from-attitudes-and-values-not-feelings-the-roots

Bancroft, L. (2003). *Why does he do that?: Inside the minds of angry and controlling men.* Penguin Publishing Group.

Beery, A. K., & Kaufer, D. (2015). Stress, social behavior, and resilience: Insights from rodents. *Neurobiology of Stress, 1*, 116–127. https://doi.org/10.1016/j.ynstr.2014.10.004

Bernet, W., Gregory, N., Rohner, R. P., & Reay, K. M. (2020). Measuring the difference between parental alienation and parental estrangement: The PARQ-Gap. *Journal of Forensic Sciences, 65*(4). https://doi.org/10.1111/1556-4029.14300

Boyd, G. (1992). *When you grow up in a dysfunctional family.* Mudrasham Institute of Spiritual Studies.

https://www.mudrashram.com/when-you-grow-up-in-a-dysfunctional-family-2/

Brummelman, E., Thomaes, S., Nelemans, S. A., Orobio de Castro, B., Overbeek, G., & Bushman, B. J. (2015). Origins of narcissism in children. *Proceedings of the National Academy of Sciences, 112*(12), 3659–3662. https://doi.org/10.1073/pnas.1420870112

Coelho, P. (n.d.). *Paolo Coelho quote.* Goodreads. https://www.goodreads.com/quotes/7634880-maybe-the-journey-isn-t-so-much-about-becoming-anything-maybe

Dantchev, S., Hickman, M., Heron, J., Zammit, S., & Wolke, D. (2019). The Independent and cumulative effects of sibling and peer bullying in childhood on depression, anxiety, suicidal ideation, and self-harm in adulthood. *Frontiers in Psychiatry, 10.* https://doi.org/10.3389/fpsyt.2019.00651

Day, N. J. S., Bourke, M. E., Townsend, M. L., & Grenyer, B. F. S. (2019). Pathological narcissism: A study of burden on partners and family. *Journal of Personality Disorders, 34*(6), 1–15. https://doi.org/10.1521/pedi_2019_33_413

Dentale, F., Verrastro, V., Petruccelli, I., Diotaiuti, P., Petruccelli, F., Cappelli, L., & Martini, P. (2015). Relationship between parental narcissism and children's mental vulnerability: Mediation role of rearing style. *International Journal of Psychology and Psychological Therapy, 15*, 337–347.

Efthim PW, Kenny ME, Mahalik JR. (2001). Gender role stress in relation to shame, guilt, and externalization. *Journal of Counseling & Development, 79*(4), 430–438. https://psycnet.apa.org/doi/10.1002/j.1556-6676.2001.tb01990.x

Fergusson, D. M. , McLeod, G. F. H. , & Horwood, L. J. (2013). Childhood sexual abuse and adult developmental outcomes: Findings from a 30-year longitudinal study in New Zealand. *Child Abuse & Neglect, 37*, 664–674. https://doi.org/10.1016/j.chiabu.2013.03.013

Gunderson, J. G., & Lyons-Ruth, K. (2008). BPD's interpersonal hypersensitivity phenotype: A gene-environment-developmental model. *Journal of Personality Disorders*, *22*(1), 22–41. https://doi.org/10.1521/pedi.2008.22.1.22

Harrison, B. G. (n.d.). *Barbara Grizzuti Harrison quote.* Quotefancy. https://quotefancy.com/quote/1227510/Barbara-Grizzuti-Harrison-My-mother-was-my-first-jealous-lover

Horton, R. S., & Tritch, T. (2013). Clarifying the links between grandiose narcissism and parenting. *The Journal of Psychology*, *148*(2), 133–143. https://doi.org/10.1080/00223980.2012.752337

Jabeen, S., Mushtaq, M., & Shahid, A. (2023). Social interaction anxiety, social isolation, self-efficacy, and depression in social networking users. *Journal of Professional & Applied Psychology*, *4*(3), 308–322. https://doi.org/10.52053/jpap.v4i3.223

Kacel, E. L., Ennis, N., & Pereira, D. B. (2017). Narcissistic personality disorder in clinical health psychology practice: Case studies of comorbid psychological distress and life-limiting illness. *Behavioral Medicine*, 43(3), 156–164. https://doi.org/10.1080/08964289.2017.1301875

Katz, E. (2016). Beyond the physical incident model: How children living with domestic violence are harmed by and resist regimes of coercive control. *Child Abuse Review*, 25(1), 46–59. https://doi.org/10.1002/car.2422

Keller, P. S., Blincoe, S., Gilbert, L. R., Dewall, C. N., Haak, E. A., & Widiger, T. (2014). Narcissism in romantic relationships: A dyadic perspective. *Journal of Social and Clinical Psychology*, *33*(1), 25–50. https://doi.org/10.1521/jscp.2014.33.1.25

Lourie, S. (2024). *The power of mess: A guide to finding joy and resilience when life feels chaotic.* Yellow Kite.

Neff, K. D. (2011). Self-compassion, self-esteem, and well-being. *Social and Personality Psychology Compass*, *5*(1), 1–12. https://doi.org/10.1111/j.1751-9004.2010.00330.x

Nietzsche, F. (n.d.). *Friedrich Nietzsche quote.* Goodreads. https://www.goodreads.com/quotes/643049-one-must-be-a-sea-to-receive-a-polluted-stream

Nolte, D. (n.d.). *Author Dorothy Law Nolte.* Children Learn What They Live. https://childrenlearnwhattheylive.com/

Rilke, R. M. (n.d.). *Rainer Maria Rilke quote.* Goodreads. https://www.goodreads.com/quotes/95915-let-everything-happen-to-you-beauty-and-terror-just-keep

Salmahnsohn, K. (2016, September 23). *"You will be too much for some people"* [Image attached] [Post]. Instagram. https://www.instagram.com/notsalmon/p/BKrjLV6BfwM/

Schoppe-Sullivan, S. J., Coleman, J., Wang, J., & Yan, J. J. (2023). Mothers' attributions for estrangement from their adult children. *Couple and Family Psychology: Research and Practice, 12*(3), 146–154. https://doi.org/10.1037/cfp0000198

Shaw, D. (2014). *Traumatic narcissism: Relational systems of subjugation.* Routledge, Taylor & Francis Group.

Stinson, F. S., Dawson, D. A., Golstein, R. B., Chou, P., Huang, B., Smith, S. M., Ruan, W. J., Pulay, A. J., Saha, T. D., Pickering, R. P., & Grant, B. F. (2008). Prevalence, correlates, disability, and comorbidity of DSM-IV narcissistic personality disorder. *The Journal of Clinical Psychiatry, 69*(7), 1033–1045. https://doi.org/10.4088/jcp.v69n0701

Swift, T. (2012). We are never ever getting back together [Song]. On *Red.* Big Machine Records.

Swift, T. (2022). The great war [Song]. On *Midnights* (3am edition). Republic Records.

Verrocchio, M. C., & Baker, A. J. L. (2015). Italian adults' recall of childhood exposure to parental loyalty conflicts. *Journal of Child and Family Studies, 24*, 95–105. https://doi.org/10.1007/s10826-013-9816-0

Waikamp, V., Serralta, F., Ramos-Lima, L. F., Zatti, C., & Freitas, L. (2021). Relationship between childhood trauma, parental bonding and defensive styles with psychiatric symptoms in the adult life. *Trends in Psychiatry and Psychotherapy*, *43*(3). https://doi.org/10.47626/2237-6089-2020-0086

Waheed, N. (n.d.). *Nayyirah Waheed quote*. Goodreads. https://www.goodreads.com/quotes/1466909-i-am-mine-before-i-am-ever-anyone-else-s

Weir, K. (2014). The lasting impact of neglect. *Monitor on Psychology*, 45(6), 36. https://www.apa.org/monitor/2014/06/neglect

Yip J., Ehrhardt K., Black H., Walker D. O. (2018). Attachment theory at work: A review and directions for future research. *Journal of Organizational Behavior*, *39*(2), 185–198. https://doi.org/10.52053/jpap.v4i3.223

Young, J. E., Klosko, J. S., & Weishaar, M. E. (2003). *Schema therapy: A practitioner's guide*. Guilford.

Made in United States
Orlando, FL
10 November 2024

53662436R00065